CRUISING BETWEEN BUENOS AIRES AND VALPARAISO
2018-19

CONTENTS

INTRODUCTION

The continent of South America, although smaller than North America, is still a vast landmass covering over 15,540,000 square kilometers or 6,000,000 square miles. There are 12 independent nations and one foreign held colony occupying the continent, with the nation of Brazil accounting for nearly half of the land area and population. But when it comes to prosperity and the level of economic development that we outsiders view as representing the first world, only Argentina, Uruguay and Chile appear to qualify based upon our own rigid criteria. Brazil is rapidly developing its industrial and agricultural infrastructure, but like México, it still suffers from massive poverty and governmental corruption. Hosting the World Cup in 2014 and the summer Olympic games in 2016 did focus both positive and negative attention on Brazil. The age-old problems of inequality, governmental corruption and crime haunt the country, and despite the Olympic games, little changed for the average resident. Argentina, Uruguay and Chile have an entirely different social and economic complexion, and these countries offer a much more developed infrastructure than anywhere else on the continent. They also differ greatly from the other South American nations, and North American or European visitors feel so much more at home. Yet in Argentina, there have been many problems involving government corruption, illegal migrants flooding in from Bolivia and declines in the overall standard of living. But unlike Brazil, Argentina still offers the visitor a much safer environment, and presents a more European atmosphere where visitors find it easier to relate.

Argentina, Uruguay and Chile evolved along totally different historical lines, and in each nation the population base is primarily European. In all three countries there is a strong mix of people from the Mediterranean, central and eastern portions of Europe, and the overall population base shows little to no mixing with the indigenous peoples who were here at the time of original colonization. Thus these countries share more of a commonality with the United States and Canada and less with the other countries of Latin America where there is a strong mix of indigenous-European and African ethnic/racial lines.

The physical environments of Argentina, Uruguay and Chile are also similar to many of the landscapes found in North America, as these countries occupy latitudes that extend from the subtropical through mid latitudes into colder reaches that almost border being sub polar. This is atypical for South America, a continent whose remaining countries all share environments that would be classified as tropical. And it is these dramatic landscapes that attracted settlers from the northern European countries. Today they attract large numbers of visitors from North America and Europe.

But like the rest of Latin America, these countries have seen explosive episodes in their history. Revolutions, counter-revolutions and popular uprisings of the masses have led to many episodes of turbulence, as recently as the late 20th century. Only in recent years have democratic principles settled in, allowing each country to concentrate upon its economic development.

This updated traveler's companion is designed for those visitors who plan to travel between Buenos Aires and Valparaiso, exploring the magnificent scenery of southern Argentina and Chile, especially the fjord country, which is so much like Alaska or Norway. Uruguay is small and very much like the flat Pampas region around Buenos Aires, but its coastal margins offer a mix of rich historic architecture, vineyards and beautiful beaches. You will find that Argentina and Chile are exceptionally spectacular countries with regard to physical landscapes, and modern countries with regard to their infrastructure. They are the most often visited of South American nations and cruises through the southern fjords enable visitors from the Northern Hemisphere to experience breathtaking scenery during the northern winter months, which is of course summer in the Southern Hemisphere. If you have visited the fjords of Norway, you must also see the beautiful fjord country of southern Argentina and Chile. The natural landscapes are absolutely spectacular. There are strong similarities to Norway, yet very major differences in both the natural landscape and the culture exist.

I trust that this traveler's companion will be beneficial in helping you to become acquainted with the landscapes, history and cultures of the three countries to be visited. Many cruise lines offer more extended circumnavigations of the South American continent, but it is the route between Buenos Aires and Valparaiso that is the most popular because of its unimaginable beauty and cool summer weather, standing in stark contrast to the rest of the continent.

This is not a typical guidebook such as Fyodor's or Frommers. You will find only limited restaurant or hotel recommendations based upon my personal experiences. The focus is to describe each of the potential ports of call and show you their major highlights, along with a brief history so you can understand and appreciate their role in each country. The primary focus of this book is to offer you an overall introduction to the lands and peoples you will be seeing to help you maximize your visit. But it leaves the ultimate choices as to what to see and do to you, as it should.

Lew Deitch
January 2018

**Visit my web site for other publications
and a beautiful around the world slide show
http://www.doctorlew.com**

A General Physical Political Map of South America based upon satellite imagery

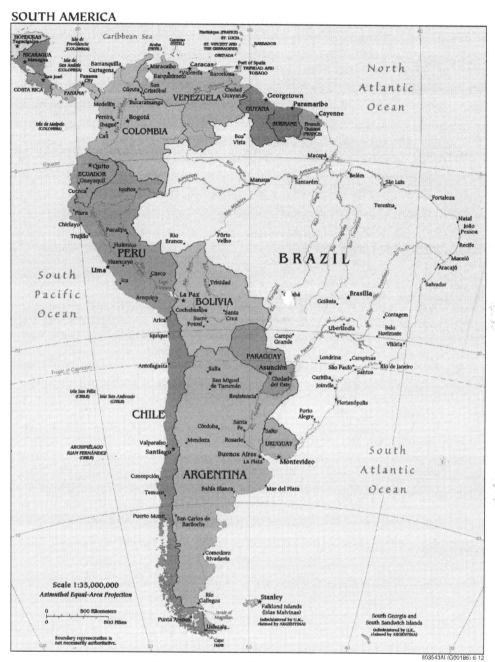

The Nations of South America

PREPARING TO CRUISE

It is astounding how many North Americans and Europeans have traveled extensively in the rest of the world, but have essentially ignored South America. There has been a sense of trepidation among many because of the violent histories and the dictatorial forms of government that have dominated the continent's history. Likewise the illegal traffic in drugs also adds to the fear of becoming a victim of crime if one travels to South America. Many of these beliefs are to a certain degree true in many of the countries of South America, but definitely not for Argentina, Uruguay or Chile. These countries with their strong European cultural base have the most well developed economies, the least amount of poverty or corruption and they are as safe for visitors as the majority of countries in Europe.

This traveler's companion has been prepared for those who are planning to cruise what is sometimes called the Southern Cone, the narrow portion of South America that is located in the middle latitudes and is known for its exceptional scenic beauty, cool summer weather and inviting ports of call.

What do you need to do to prepare for your cruise? This question involves numerous sub topics that will be explained. There are many questions people have regarding visas, the long flight over, what to pack with regard to weather conditions, currency issues and health concerns. I will address many of those issues here. If you have specific and personalized questions, please contact me at my web page and I will respond with answers to your personal questions. The web site is http://www.info@doctorlew.com.

VISAS: Chile and Uruguay do not require a visa for visits up to 90 days for passport holders from the United States, Canada and members of the European Union. It is imperative that you check with your cruise line for specific details, as visa requirements often change without advanced notice. Argentina does require a reciprocity fee of $160.00 for residents of the United States, which must be handled on line at the Provincia Pagos website, www.reciprocidad.provincianet.com.ar. This is not a visa, but a fee that must be paid prior to entry to Argentina if you are flying in and starting your cruise in Buenos Aires. If you are entering by ship at the end of your cruise and then flying out of the country, the fee needs to also be paid, and should be taken care of before entry into the country. Again it is vital to contact your cruise line for specific details, as many lines work in conjunction with visa service companies that can expedite the matter. This fee may also be charged to citizens of other nations where a visa is not required, but the fee is still necessary to be paid.

Although Chile does not require a visa, an entry permit is issued upon arrival. This card must be kept with your passport and then surrendered at the time of departure. If the card is lost, there will be a fee for a replacement. If the card should be stolen, the International Police of Chile at www.investigaciones.cl must issue its replacement. Once again, it is imperative that you check with your cruise line because requirements can change without notice.

THE LONG FLIGHT: It does not matter if you are coming from North America or Europe; the flight to South America is long. From the United States or Canada there are direct flights to Buenos Aires and Santiago. From Santiago it is necessary to get to the ship in Valparaiso, which is about 112 kilometers or 70 miles to the west, but most cruise lines do provide group transfers. In Buenos Aires, the cruise terminal is just a few kilometers from the city center where most of the first class hotels are located. If you prefer a private transfer, ask your cruise line representative to arrange a private transfer.

Flights from North America to either Buenos Aires or Santiago take anywhere from ten to 13 hours depending upon the point of origin. Miami and Dallas are closer to South America than New York or Toronto. In all cases, the flights are overnight and there are no major time zone changes coming from North America, so that helps eliminate much of the jet lag factor. Buenos Aires is in the GMT-3 time zone equal to that of Greenland Standard Time. Santiago is in the GMT-4 time zone equal to that of Atlantic Standard Time in eastern Canada.

Flights from European cities such as London, Paris, Frankfurt or Zurich take around 14 hours, and flying westward, you loose time, which can compound the jet lag factor because your body's internal clock is reading anywhere from three to five hours behind, depending upon the city from which you departed.

I highly recommend Business Class because most airlines today offer the full flat beds, which are so much more comfortable than being in coach or even the upgraded coach class. Yes it is more expensive, but there are non-refundable Business Class fares if you purchase well ahead of traveling. Check with the airline regarding the configuration of the Business Class cabin, as some offer a greater degree of space and privacy than others. The new Boeing 787, called the Dreamliner, has so many amenities that it truly is superior to all other aircraft.

Upon arrival in or departure from either Buenos Aires or Santiago, I strongly urge that you spend a few days to enjoy each of these dynamic capital cities. Farther into the text, I do have detailed chapters on both Buenos Aires and Santiago in which I point out all of the exciting features of each city. These are two of the most distinctive and progressive cities in South America and neither should be missed. You will cheat yourself out of a great experience if you miss either city. You should preferably spend time in both.

WEATHER: Most cruises around the lower end of South America occur during the Southern Hemisphere summer, which would include the months of December through March. Buenos Aires has a humid subtropical climate, and it can be quite war and sticky from Christmas to the end of March. The weather conditions would be comparable to those of Charleston, South Carolina in the southern United States. Santiago has a drier Mediterranean type climate, which during their summer is very much like that of Los Angeles, California.

But as you go south, the temperatures begin to drop, and the westerly winds pick up to where it can be quite chilly and windy by the time you reach the Straits of Magellan. And snow squalls can occur even in the middle of summer. A warm jacket, hat, gloves and scarf are recommended if you want to stay on deck while sailing through the straits and down to Ushuaia or around Cape Horn (weather permitting). The last time I was in Ushuaia, it had snowed the night before, so even though it was December, it was the equivalent of snow in June in the Northern Hemisphere. If your cruise also includes the detour out to the Falkland Islands, be prepared for chilly, windy weather most of the time, if you even get there, as the seas can be exceptionally rough between the mainland and the Falklands.

Coming north or south along the Pacific Coast, the weather will remain quite cool and often blustery until you reach the Chileno Lake District. Here temperatures will be in the low to mid 20's Celsius or 70's Fahrenheit and quite pleasant. Then as the ship travels north to Valparaiso, the temperatures will warm and the humidity will drop. Valparaiso and Santiago have a warm, dry summer climate that is classified as Mediterranean by climatologists. This of course means warm to hot sunny weather and little or no chance of rain. But once again, if you take a tour into the Andes while staying in Santiago, you will need a moderate weight jacket. Some of the mountain resorts in Chile are at over 3,050 meters or 10,000 feet in altitude. Although the sun may feel hot on your face because of the rarified atmosphere, the ambient temperature could be in the 40's or 50's during the day and drop below freezing at night even in mid summer.

WHAT TO PACK: You will need casual clothes for on board ship and for sightseeing, with layers preferable. Warmer shirts, sweaters, scarves and gloves are advisable along with a warm windproof jacket. But in the Santiago and Buenos Aires areas, you will want to be cool and comfortable. In the cities, few locals wear shorts or T-shirts. That is definitely the mark of an American tourist. At the beach resorts shorts and T-shirts are the norm.

On board ship, especially while in the southern waters around the southern fjords and Tierra del Fuego the air can get chilly out on deck, especially in the evenings. And in December, snow is always possible. I know it sounds normal from a Northern Hemisphere perspective, but remember that snow in December is like saying snow in June back home.

Depending upon your cruise line, evening attire of a more formal nature may be required. And in Buenos Aires and Santiago people do tend to dress in smart casual attire when they go out for dinner at most restaurants. In these countries dining out in the evening is similar to that of Spain. Most people arrive at a restaurant for dinner after nine or ten in the evening.

CURRENCY: You will need to change your dollars, Pounds or Euro for the local currency of each country. All three countries use a unit of currency called the peso. But each country has its own banking system and issues its own banknotes and coins. Thus you will use the Argentine Peso, the Uruguayan Peso and the Chileno Peso.

The Falkland Islands are a British colony, and they mint their own version of the pound, known as the Falkland Island Pound.

Most establishments will not accept foreign currency. And to exchange at a currency exchange booth (cambio), you generally are required to show your passport.

POSTAGE: If you wish to send post cards or letters you are best doing it on board the ship. But even in so doing, there is only a fifty percent chance that the mail will be received at its final destination. The postal systems are not that reliable when it comes to international mail. You will be better served using e-mail.

LOCAL ELECTRICITY: In all South American countries, the voltage is 220, as it is in Europe and Australia. If you have electric appliances such as a hair dryer or toothbrush, you may need to purchase an adapter if you are planning to stay in a hotel prior to or following the cruise. Many hotels do have 110 voltage plugs, and in that case you do not need to purchase the adapter.

LANDSCAPES OF ARGENTINA

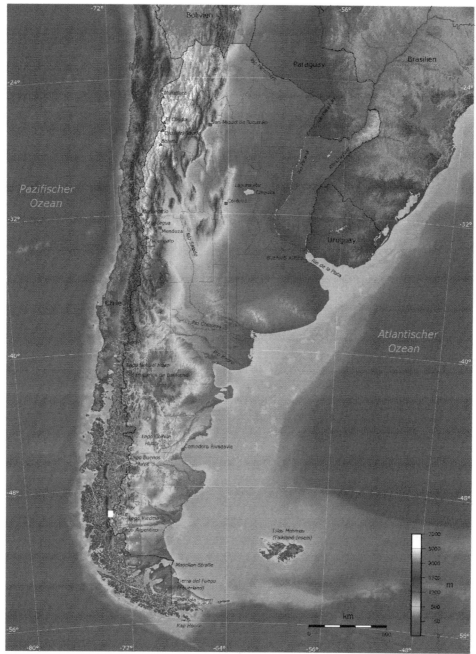

Shaded relief map of Argentina (Work of Captain Blood, CC BY SA 3.0, Wikimedia.org)

There are many superlatives that apply to the physical landscapes of Argentina. This is a nation of magnificent beauty as you travel from one breathtaking vista to another. The landscapes are diverse, varying from some of the highest mountains in the world to vast, open plains that stretch as far as the eye can see. The land also varies with regard to vegetation and climate, being sub tropical in the far north and sub polar in the far south.

Argentina is a large country, occupying 2,780,398 square kilometers or 1,073,518 square miles. By comparison, this is approximately six and one half times the size of the American state of California. In physical size Argentina is the second largest country in all of Latin America in land area. The country tapers in width from around 1,000 kilometers or 600 miles in the north to only 160 kilometers or 100 miles in the far south, but Argentina stretches over 3,000 kilometers or 2,000 miles in length. Because the country is so much longer than it is wide, it occupies only one time zone, that of GMT-3, placing it two hours later than Eastern Standard Time in the United States.

Argentina is not an overly populated country. The last estimate of population in 2012 placed the nation at 43,431,0000, just slightly greater than the population of California or Canada. Given that nearly 15,200,000 people live in the capital city of Buenos Aires, this leaves a moderate population to scatter over the vastness of the country, leaving many areas essentially empty.

The eastern rim of the country, forming a natural boundary with Chile and Bolivia, consists of the Andes Mountains. These are the longest mountain ranges on earth, and also the second highest. The entire boundary from northeast to far south consists of an unbroken wall of up faulted and volcanic mountains, the highest peaks being in the central portion of the border with Chile. Mt. Aconcagua at 6,960 meters or 22,834 feet is the highest mountain in the Western Hemisphere and one of the ten highest mountain peaks in the entire world. The Andes rise as jagged crags, punctuated by individual volcanic cones primarily in the southern portion of the range. These mountains receive heavy snowfall and contain numerous glaciers, presenting not only a magnificent landscape, but also a formidable barrier to transportation. The sheer face of the mountains on both the eastern and western faces, with few foothill regions makes the Andes a dramatic mountain range that towers above the surrounding lowlands on the east and west. The mountain barrier has enabled the cultures of each country to develop quite independent of the other because of the difficulty in communicating that was even more pronounced in the days before modern transportation.

Most of the mountain slopes are too sheer to support vegetation, but in the lower flanks, especially to the south, there are thick forests of southern beech and other broadleaf evergreen species. However, in the middle latitudes the prevailing winds blow off the Pacific Ocean, thus placing the Argentine slopes in the rain shadow, limiting the development of forests to the narrow valleys and marginal foothills in the immediate shadow of the higher peaks. Above these forests there is a region of deciduous stunted trees and shrubs that does present brilliant displays of autumn coloring from mid April into early May. Remember that here in the Southern Hemisphere seasons are reversed from what we are familiar with. Winter comes during June through August, and it does bring heavy snow to the upper peaks of the entire Andean range, but snow also falls on the lower slopes and out onto the plains in southern Argentina.

To the north, the leeward slopes are drier, even to the extent of presenting a desert environment known as the Puna, extending from Tucumán north to the border of Bolivia. Here the land is essentially cloaked in scrub and grasses, with a scattering of tall trichocereus cacti, similar in nature to the North American Saguaro, but not quite as large and containing longer, soft looking thorns.

In the southern portion of the Andean ranges, along the border with Chile, the mountains experienced intense glaciations during the Pleistocene, leaving behind two remnant glacial fields and a plethora of deep, crystal clear lakes. This region, which is found in both countries, is known as the Lake District. Interspersed between the lakes are snow capped, sheer volcanic cones. The combination of volcanoes, lakes and thick forests makes this one of the most scenic of regions in South America. This is also a popular winter recreation region, especially focused upon the city of Bariloche. The quality of the snow and the facilities both would warrant being chosen for the winter Olympic games, but the time of the year would not be conducive to holding the games since most winter athletes are accustomed to Northern Hemisphere winter and would not be in peak training during what we in the north consider to be summer.

There are very few passes through the Andes that connect Argentina and Chile, the main route for both highway and railway connection between Buenos Aires and Santiago being just to south of Mt.

Aconcagua. This highway is known as the Carretera Internacional and it is a torturous road that takes a lot of physical nerve to drive. Farther south, only minor roads link the two countries in a handful of locations. The same is true farther north, thus essentially isolating Argentina from its neighbor Chile with whom it shares so much today on an economic basis.

The land falls away to the east of the Andes, becoming essentially a landscape of level to gently rolling land. In the rain shadow of the Andes, the landscape is essentially a semi-arid steppe that becomes increasingly arid to the north because of the scant amount of moisture that comes into northern Chile's Atacama Desert. This is the result of the cold Humboldt Current that wells up and limits the amount of evaporation from the surface of the sea. But there is sufficient moisture falling at the highest elevations in the form of snow to create rivers that flow both into Argentina and westward into Chile, allowing for limited agriculture along their banks.

In the center of the country, the Pampas forms the most important geographic region of Argentina. Stretching eastward from the foothill city of Mendoza, the Pampas are the Great Plains of Argentina. This mid latitude grassland is home to the country's massive cattle ranches known as estancias. It was the great ranches that made Argentina economically and politically. Ranches and large wheat farms mirrored the historic development of the Great Plains of the United States. With a similar geographic environment, the same types of grain farming and ranching developed, but with a slightly different cultural twist as will be discussed later in the text. The Pampas stretch all the way to the great estuary known as the Rio de la Plata, which is the mouth of the Rio Paraná. Although not as large as the North American Great Plains, the Pampas region is the breadbasket of Argentina and provides the country with its most valuable exports – grains and beef. The ranches developed on this fertile land and grew into major estancias, each with its own community of workers and often its own traditions. The famous Gaucho, or Argentine cowboy, developed his lifestyle on these massive ranches.

Argentina's heaviest population is found on the Pampas, including the national capital city of Buenos Aires. Essentially the great agricultural and ranching hinterland created the city, as it became the major port for the exporting of the vast quantities of grain and meat that became so important to Argentina. All of the country's rail lines and major highways radiate outward from Buenos Aires across the Pampas, becoming thinner as the distance increases outward. In Many ways there is a similarity to the way in which railway and highway routes fan out to the west from Chicago across the North American Great Plains.

To the north, The Pampas grade into a region of sub tropical scrub woodland known as the Gran Chaco. This is a difficult land to occupy, as the scrub country is difficult to clear, and its fertility once cleared is less than desirable. This is also a region with two distinct seasons – wet and dry occur, again making agriculture and ranching difficult. But there have been those who have settled in this land and been successful with a lot of hard work. As one moves westward toward the Andes, the Gran Chaco dries out to almost become a semi-arid steppe, but as one moves east toward the border of Brazil, the Gran Chaco receives over 20 inches of precipitation, and it is especially green during the wet season.

The most dramatic feature to be found in the Gran Chaco is Iguaçu Falls, located along the Rio Paraná on the border between Argentina, Brazil and Paraguay. This rather remote waterfall is second only to the great Victoria Falls of Africa. It is a mighty series of cascades whose spray can be seen for miles and whose thunder creates such a roar that one can feel it in their very bones. Although remote, there are good hotels since this is a world famous tourist attraction. The falls are also connected to Buenos Aires and Rio de Janeiro by direct air service.

The southern third of Argentina, east of the Andes is known as Patagonia. This is an increasingly cold, windswept and semi arid land as one proceeds to the south. The prevailing winds off the high Andes bring little moisture, as it is primarily squeezed out of the atmosphere by the high peaks. Patagonia is located in the belt of the westerly winds, but on the leeward side of the world's second highest mountains. Thus the semi arid grass and scrubland extends right down to the shores of the South Atlantic Ocean. Ranching is the primary activity in this part of the country, and only the heartiest of settlers have made Patagonia home. But it is also a majestic land, especially in the far south because Patagonia is narrow, and one is seldom out of sight of the towering, snow draped Andes. Tourists are discovering this region, rich in bird life with its offshore waters teeming in seals, whales and penguins. It is truly a naturalist's paradise. And in the lower slopes of the Andes there are still active glaciers whose melt water has created sparkling blue lakes.

Argentina possesses an extensive coastline, fronting only on the South Atlantic Ocean. There are many deep-water harbors, but below the Pampas, there is so little in the way of economic development that these harbors are for the most part left in a pristine state. Thus most of the south coast is a haven for wildlife, still largely unspoiled. Argentina and Chile both occupy the large island at the far south end of the continent known as Tierra del Fuego. The shoreline of the mainland and the island both shows many deep fjords as a result of glaciation. Separating Tierra del Fuego from the mainland are the Straits of Magellan, an interior passage that enabled ships to transition between the South Atlantic and South Pacific Oceans without going around the south end of Tierra del Fuego and risking the intense storms of Cape Horn. Once discovered, the Straits of Magellan became the primary route between the east and west coasts of the United States until the opening of the Panama Canal. Today ships still ply these waters, but only those too large to use the canal. When it was completed in Norfolk, Virginia, the United States aircraft carrier U. S. S. Ronald Reagan used the straits when the ship was assigned from Norfolk to San Diego.

Summer cruises around the southern end of the continent are now also a popular event for foreign tourists, summer season being December through March. And it is this region that will become the focus for this traveler's companion, as it is here that the scenery reaches its peak of magnificence. The island's indented coastline has created fjords that rival those of Alaska for their scenic quality. And the mountains rise in jagged peaks and towers, giving the land an almost primeval look. There is a major ice field that still sends active glaciers down to the sea. In the Straits of Magellan the landscape is equally as pristine and magnificent, and it opens into the interior passages between the mainland and offshore islands providing for sheltered travel far north along the coast of Chile. Each year tens of thousands of cruisers are exposed to a landscape of magnificent vistas not spoiled by human development.

Aconcagua is the highest peak of the Andes (Work of Mario Roberto Duran Ortiz, CC BY SA 3.0, Wikimedia.org)

The southern Andes reach into a sub polar climate on Tierra del Fuego

The Lake District around Bariloche (Work of Nooperation, CC BY SA 4.0, Wikimedia.org)s

Along the edge of the high Andes in the north (Work of CarlosA.Barrio, CC BY SA 4.0, Wikimedia.org)

The semi-arid Andean foothills in the northern state of Salta (Work of CarlosA.Barrio, CC BY SA 40, Wikimedia.org)

The sub tropical landscape of the Gran Chaco (Work of Pertile, CC BY SA 3.0, Wikimedia.org)

The rich agriculture of the Pampas (Work of Germanramos, CC BY SA 3.0, Wikimedia.org)

The cold, semi-arid lands of Patagonia in the south (Work of Justraveling.com, CC BY SA 4.0, Wikimedia.org)

The dramatic and magnificent Iguacu Falls in the northeast

Iguacu Falls are hard to believe until you see them yourself.

ARGENTINE HISTORY & POLITICS

Argentina is a country whose history and politics can be summarized by one word – turbulent. This may be true for many countries, but it is especially so for Argentine. Many political analysts say that the Argentine psyche is one that thrives on turmoil, as the people have shown a penchant for revolution. Although the population is primarily of European stock, prior to colonization there was an extensive native population, thus our history lesson must begin with a discussion of the indigenous peoples.

There were numerous hunting and gathering tribes scattered across Argentina, but there were also two primary farming peoples, the Diaguita in the northwest and the Guarani in what is now known as the Pampas. Both peoples lived in small villages and raised corn and vegetables, similar to many of the farming peoples of the Mesoamerica. However, the Diaguita were also good warriors and ultimately prevented the Inca Empire from expanding southward through the few mountain passes into what is now Argentina. Ultimately introduced European diseases combined with continued warfare decimated the native population. By the 19th century, the indigenous population was essentially reduced to minimal levels, and today there are only a few villages where pureblooded native peoples can be found, primarily in the Andean foothills of Patagonia. In essence, the native people have almost been forgotten as ever having inhabited the land.

When the Spanish first discovered the coast of Argentina and attempted to colonize, their efforts were met by hostility. From 1516 until the latter years of the 16th century, settlement was essentially impossible. By 1580, however, Buenos Aires was established as a port and trade center, but Spain essentially forbade trade with other nations. Buenos Aires ultimately languished and became a haven for smugglers. Inland colonies based their settlement upon limited ranching and the mining of silver, but they were more closely tied to Bolivia and Peru over the northwestern mountain passes. The name Argentina comes from the early mining of silver, which in Latin is called argentium.

British naval forces attacked Buenos Aires in 1806 and again in 1807, as Spain had come under Napoleonic rule. The colonials fended off the British without any assistance from Spanish forces still loyal to King Ferdinand VII. However, after the king's capture by the French, this put Argentina under the direct rule of a viceroy appointed by the Napoleonic government. After the fall of Napoleon, and the restoration of the Spanish crown, the people of Argentina grew restive with regard to being a colony. Rebellion culminated in 1816 with the Argentine people declaring their independence. Under the leadership of General José de San Marin, the country won its independence. San Marin and fellow revolutionary leader Simon Bolivar in the northern Andean region ultimately broke Spain's hold on South America. To this day, the name of San Martin is revered in Argentina as the father of the nation. There are statues of him in every major city, and he is considered to be the great national hero very much like George Washington in the United States.

The original nation occupied only the area surrounding Buenos Aires, but by the 1850's, territorial growth created Argentina as we see it today. After achieving independence, a pattern of internal discontent began to set the stage for what has been until the last three decades the hallmark of Argentine politics. Just as in the United States, two factions developed, one favoring a strong central government (Unitarists) and those wanting more local control (Federalists). In the early years, the country was ruled over by a succession of dictators who plunged the country into periods of turmoil. Americans resolved differences through the development of a strong constitution to which the leaders are sworn to uphold, although the Civil War did occur because the Constitution had not settled the issue of slavery. The Argentine people have not been as faithful to their constitution, which they did not adopt until 1853, when a republic with elected leadership was ultimately declared. But that would not be the end to dictatorial rule or military intervention as will be seen.

The greatest influences in Argentina came from the waves of immigration, which essentially brought a European cultural matrix to its shores. Basque separatists came from Spain, choosing to settle primarily in the windswept lands of Patagonia. Irish peasants escaping the potato famine came and settled wherever they could obtain farmland. Welsh miners and farmers came, settling where they could find work or land. Italian and German immigrants came, primarily settling in the Andean foothills. All the while, British investors poured money into the country to develop its railroads and limited industries, primarily because Argentina looked to be a great storehouse of minerals and agricultural products, items needed by the British Empire. Jewish immigrants settled in Buenos Aires and the other major cities, and there are even small communities of Japanese farmers scattered across the country. Ultimately this melting pot of people accepted their new homeland, learned Spanish and became Argentine, but many still retained ties to their families back home. But of course in many communities, people continued to use their ancestral language at home, while Spanish remained the language of the street for business and education. Again the parallel to 19th century American immigration shows that Argentina is a country with close ties to its predominantly European roots. All the while, the native people diminished in number. Immigrants from neighboring countries also moved into Argentina, adding further to the overall cultural matrix. This combination of talent, along with British and other foreign investment made Argentina the strongest economic force in South America by the start of the 20th century.

During World War I, Argentina remained neutral despite its strong European ties to both sides of the conflict. The country proved to be a valuable source of food and raw material, as the government permitted extensive trade with the western allied governments. Following the war, Argentina did not fare as well. With the world plunged into depression, there were few markets for Argentine products, thus the country was also plunged into depression with high unemployment and social unrest. Like in Germany and Italy, Argentina saw the rise of Fascist movements, which came to a head in 1938 when President Roberto Ortiz proclaimed the country's neutrality at the outbreak of World War II. With its large German and Italian population now one to two generations removed, there was still surprisingly strong sympathy for the Axis. A 1943 military coup turned the country pro western, breaking diplomatic ties with Germany, Italy and Japan, but this quickly led to a counter coup led by Colonel Juan Perón, a charismatic leader who did admire many attributes of the Nazi cause. In the new government that he helped inaugurate, he became the powerful Minister of Labor, a position that gave him access to the working classes. Seeing that the war was going against the Axis, and fearing a loss of Allied markets, Argentina declared war on Germany and Japan in early 1945, but the country's gesture was only that. But it saved the country from being shunned by the Allied powers. As a further gesture of its solidarity with the Allied cause, Argentina joined the United Nations as a charter member in late 1945.

Following the war, the country entered one of its most intoxicating eras. Juan Perón had captivated the working classes, especially with the aid of his elegant and beautiful wife Eva. A pro Perón movement, known as the Peronistas, swept him into power as an elected president in 1946 on the promise that he would improve life for the working classes. His government initiated many industrial expansion programs by encouraging corporate investment, and he appropriated money to build schools, sports facilities and other amenities for the public. Eva would listen to the woes of thousands of peasants, handing out quantities of pesos to those in need. They both became endeared to the masses, and this allowed him to push through a new constitution in 1949, which allowed an elected president to run again for office. In 1952, he won reelection with the massive support of the working classes. However, there was opposition among the industrialists, journalists and upper class, which was met with repression, torture and jail sentences. The government even expropriated "La Prensa," the most influential of the Buenos Aires newspapers. A second five-year plan, this time emphasizing agricultural production did not stem the rising inflation, and this brought about disaffection. The final blow came when the Catholic Church did not support the new social legislation. The end for Perón came in 1955 when initially the navy withdrew its support, but the loyal army quickly put that down. But within a few months entire cadre of military officers forced the country into civil war. The bloodshed only lasted three days, but with thousands dead, Juan Perón saw the futility of resisting the tide against him. He resigned and went into exile in Spain. Many claim that his downfall was the death of his beloved Eva. He never regained his momentum, and the people lost faith with him after her death. She was a driving force among the masses, and her untimely death from cancer resulted in one of the largest state funerals in Latin American history. The musical Evita is based upon the story of Eva Perón who rose from the ranks of the peasantry to become the country's first lady. Her life was a tragedy, and if those of you who saw the movie recall, the theme song was "Don't Cry for Me Argentina."

The story of Juan Perón does not end with his exile. There is more. In 1956, following his departure from the country, the new president, General Leonardi was unable to suppress the Peronistas, leading to another coup d'état within two months. The new regime was military, and it quickly squelches the Perionista movement, but Juan Perón encouraged his supporters to protest by casting blank ballots in the ensuing election. The blank ballots actually exceeded the vote of any other party, but the military declared Arturo Frondizi the new president. Frondizi actually had support from many Peronistas as well as Communists, and he proceeded to restore civil government. He managed to stabilize the economy, primarily through massive foreign aid. But within less than two years, most of his supporters deserted him in favor of their own political objectives. In 1962, a military junta removed Frondizi. The generals, with the aid of Senate president José Maria Guido, ran the government until 1963 when they were persuaded by public pressure to allow national elections. By military decree, the Peronistas and Communists were barred from standing for office, thus allowing Arturo Illia to win the election, but without the support of the masses that boycotted the election. His government lasted less than one year when the military once again stepped in and removed him from office. This became a recurring theme in Argentine politics. If the military was dissatisfied, the civilian government was terminated. This is why Perón lasted so long – he was a member of the military and had their support.

By 1973, the situation had grown critical. A succession of military presidents took office from 1966 onward, but none could satisfy the generals. The public had grown increasingly restive and the Peronistas were the most violent force leading one strike and demonstration after another. In 1972, Peronistas nominate Juan Perón for president, but since he was in exile, a stand-in named Hector Cámpora was put on the ballot. He won the election with a massive plurality, and then stepped down in 1973 in favor of Juan Perón, as the party had become increasingly agitated, leading to more demonstrations for Cámpora's resignation. Juan Perón returned from Spain and requested that his new wife Isabella be named his vice president. There was jubilation in the country, but given that he was not well by this time, he died suddenly in 1974, propelling Isabella into the presidency. She was totally unprepared, and as a result her administration was a disaster, especially on the economic front. Again the military stepped in and deposed her in 1976, again placing the military generals in charge of the government. If this sounds like an endless story, it is not over yet. I had noted earlier that Argentine politics is tumultuous, and now you can start to see why.

When the military again came to power, the chosen president Lieutenant General Jorge Videla, banned labor unions, and his repressions were followed by General Roberto Viola and then by Leopoldo Galtieri, who promised to return democratic rule, but who waged a brutal war of arrest, torture and execution against thousands of citizens who protested the military's domination of the government. Most of those arrested simply disappeared, and to this day, mothers of many who were never seen again still demonstrate in front of the Casa Rosada (presidential palace) in Buenos Aires.

The ultimate indignity to Argentina came in 1982 when General Galtieri invaded the Falkland Islands in an unprovoked war that was designed to focus attention upon Argentine nationalism and distract the populace from an economy that was nearly in shambles. The British had held the Falkland Islands since the mid 19th century. These rocky, cold islands, which lie about 480 miles off the southern coast of Argentina, are only inhabited by just over 2,900 people. There is little economic value to this island group, but the Argentinos have claimed that they are rightfully theirs from back in the days when the Spanish used them for military purposes. Known to the Argentine as the Islas Malvinas, they were invaded in 1982 and quickly occupied. The British government dispatched a major fleet to rescue the islanders. The ensuing war ended in British victory and a humiliation for the government of Argentina. Today the two governments are working jointly to explore the Falkland Islands and surrounding seas for the possibility of finding oil. The defeat of the Argentine military totally discredited the military junta in power, and ultimately had the beneficial result of forcing the return to constitutional rule in 1984. As a side note - to this day when the weather news is reported on Argentine television, the Islas Malvinas weather is shown as if it were part of the country. And there are large signs around the nation that proclaim, "Islas Malvinas son Argentinas," "the Malvinas Islands are Argentine."

Raúl Alfonsín won a dramatic election campaign in 1984. But he was unable to turn around the economy, which had deteriorated to where the country's infrastructure was in jeopardy of collapse. He did, however, establish civilian control over the military, a battle that was hard fought. He also attempted to ascertain what had happened to the thousands who had disappeared under the Galtieri administration, but to that end he was not successful. In 1989, under the second consecutive free election, Carlos Menem won the presidency. He was a very popular local governor, a member of the Peronistas and a highly colorful figure who had great charisma. Menem did bring about great changes, albeit through means that were quite controversial. He even went to the point of issuing presidential decrees when the Congress could not reach agreement on his reforms. He brought about significant changes in the economy, encouraged foreign investment, restructured the national debt, sold off many government entities and stabilized the country's economy, the effects still being felt to this day. In 1995, Menem won a second term, but the remainder of his time in office ended up being a period of scandals and corruption, plus public discontent with the austerity programs he had instituted to save the country from ruin. In the 1999 election, Fernando de la Rúa, a candidate representing two opposition parties in coalition, won the presidential election, but scandal taints his administration and he is forced to resign in 2001

And so it goes with the story of Argentine history. Since Rúa's resignation, the political arena has not been very secure. A replacement, Adolfo Saa, lasted for one week, one of the shortest reigns in history. The Congress then chose an interim president, Eduardo Duhalde, who devalued the peso and continued to watch the country decline in almost a state of helplessness, hoping to win the April 2003 election, despite public displeasure. The 2003 election was won by Peronista Néstor Kirchner, which brought quite a stir to Argentina. His policies were quite a departure from the Argentine norm. He initially told the International Monetary Fund and bondholders that Argentina would not pay the large foreign debit incurred in the manner that the IMF and foreign banks were demanding. He also cracked down on the hard-core unemployed "piqueteros" who for years had used such tactics as roadblocks and seizure of government buildings to air their grievances. He forced the unemployed back to work; possibly at times performing jobs that they would not otherwise have taken. He is also took a hard line on the nation's debt, corruption and in so doing he strengthened Argentina's image, thus encouraging more foreign investment. As a Peronista, his tactics were refreshing since they were not predictable. For example as a Peronista, he supported labor's right to demonstrate, but as president, he demanded that it be orderly, reigning in the security forces and only using them if totally necessary. He courted big business interests, but he was not in their pocket. His interests appeared to be aimed at the well-being of the nation – and this was refreshing.

The president gave the country a new lease on its future. There were mixed feelings among the people, but at least foreign investment was being seen, the gross domestic product rose, and inflation had been essentially halted.

In the fall of 2005, Argentina hosted the leaders of the Western Hemisphere at a conference held in Mar del Plata. The primary purpose of the meeting was to discuss the creation of a hemispheric trade block similar to the North American Free Trade Agreement already in place. Argentine demonstrators, especially those from among the poor who have not as yet found work in the recovering economy, took to the streets in violent demonstration, some even burning and looting stores and offices. Although the burning and looting were not typical, the nature of the vocal demonstrations showed once again that Argentine people are volatile when it comes to the political scene. Much of the anger was directed at the United States, fueled by a rally held by the Venezuelan president, a man with strong Cuban and Marxist leanings, and a foe of President Bush. These demonstrations did not help Presidente Kirchner, who tried to maintain a stately manner as the summit host.

President Nestor Kirchner's wife Cristina won a major victory in October 2007, as the country's first woman president. Both Presidents Kirchner have represented the popular Peronista Party. Preidente Cristina Kirchner has continued with her husband's policies and won a second term in 2011. She has continued to face labor unrest, strikes and a declining economic base.

In 2015, Argentina held elections for president, but after two terms, Cristina Kirchner was not eligible to run again, and it is doubtful people would support her if she were to attempt to run in 2020. Under the Argentine constitution, a person can run for another two consecutive terms after being out of office for one term.

The election was held on October 25, but neither of the two front running candidates won a solid majority. Frente de la Victoria (Peronista) candidate Daniel Scioli won 37.8 percent of the vote, but his major opponent Mauricio Macri won 34.1 percent. In the November 22 run off, Mauricio Macri, the wealthy mayor of Buenos Aires defeated the Peronista Daniel Scioli. Macri pledges to build up the economy and repair the so-called damage done by the former administration, but only time will tell.

I am sure that many of you got lost in reading the brief Argentine historic sketch, but it was important, as you cannot understand what motivates the Argentine people without having some background as to their rather raucous political system. This is a country where people take politics seriously and voice their opinions in demonstrations quite easily.

What follows now is just a brief look at how the government of Argentina functions under its constitution, showing you that despite the penchant for turmoil, the country does have the potential for stability if it adheres to its constitution. Argentina is classified as a republic, similar to the United States. This means that the country possesses a constitution, a national legislature, a separate executive branch and a division of power between the federal and provincial governments. But unlike the United States, you have seen that Argentine politics have set the course on a path of instability, upheaval and revolution that is quite contrary to what the republic should experience.

Argentina is divided into 23 individual provinces, each with its own legislature and governor, similar in their level of power to that found in the United States or among the Canadian prairies.

The country celebrates Revolution Day as May 25. This dates back to 1810 when the people first rose up against Spanish rule. But independence itself did not occur until July 9, 1816. The constitution under which the country functions was not adopted until May 1, 1853. It was suspended for a period of time during military rule as noted earlier, but it was reinstated and revised in August 1994.

The President of Argentina is both the chief of state, meaning that he or she heads up the executive branch of government, as well as being the head of state. As head of state, he or she is the highest official representing Argentina in the eyes of the world. The public at large elects president, and then he or she chooses the executive cabinet to head the various departments of the government. The vice president is elected along with the president just as in the United States. The term of office is four years.

The legislature is the Congreso Nacional. It is bicameral, meaning that there are two houses. The upper house is known as the Senate, consisting of 72 members, three from each of the provinces. Until recently they were appointed by provincial legislatures. But as of 2001, the seats have been filled by open election and the term of office is six years, with one third up for election every two years. The lower house is the Chamber of Deputies and contains 257 seats spread across the provinces by population. The deputies serve for four-year terms, with half up for election every two years.

There are numerous political parties in Argentina, but the Frente de la Victoria, or modern Peronistas are still the dominant force, often holding either the largest or second largest blocks of votes. The makeup of the parties is complex, and by American standards difficult to understand. They range from conservative to outright radical in their views, one party known as the Front for a Country in Solidarity (Frepaso) is actually a four-party coalition.

The Corte Suprema, is comprised of nine justices who are appointed by the president with the approval of the Senate, just as in the United States. Below the Supreme Court, there is a complex judicial structure that ranges from regional to local courts, and on paper functions in a manner similar to that of the United States. However, no judges are elected. All serve by political appointment. The courts of Argentina are dominated over by prevailing political parties, and the concept of justice is different in practice from what it appears to be by its structure.

Just as in the United States, political action groups exert a lot of pressure upon the government. However, in Argentina one of the primary forms of political action has been and continues to be violent demonstration. Various labor unions, political action groups and even the Catholic Church organize violent protests whenever they feel the need to express discontent with the government. The most recent example of political violence occurred in early November 2005 during the summit of leaders of the Western Hemisphere. In this instance, violence also included widespread vandalism. Argentina has always been a nation of vociferous people, and that practice clearly has not changed.

This rather lengthy historical and political summary is important because even as a short-term visitor to Argentina it is necessary to grasp the impact of the political scene. Demonstrations often are sparked at a moment's notice. And the mothers of those who disappeared are still seen on a regular basis in the Plaza de Mayo in front of the Casa Rosada in Buenos Aires. In this way, you will have an understanding of the volatility of the Argentine political scene and its impact upon the nation.

General Jose de San Martin, the liberator and father of Argentina

Presidente Juan Perón, the most popular figure in modern Argentine history, and his first wife Eva who was beloved by the masses

Signs proclaiming that the Falkland Islands are still Argentine (Work of Tjeerd Wiersma, CC BY SA 2.0, Wikimedia.org)

Argentine army prisoners of war taken in the Falklands

Presidente Mauricio Macri, elected in 2016 (Casa Rosada, CC BY SA 2.5 ar, Wikimedia.org)

THE ARGENTINE LIFESTYLE

Argentina comes as a surprise to most outsiders when they first visit the country. Many tourists expect to visit a country that is similar to México. Instead they find a country that is more like Europe than it is Latin American. And this is the great paradox that is Argentina. To say that the way of life is truly European would be as incorrect as to say that its way of life is typically Latin American. It is essentially a fusion of both. To best understand this country, the lifestyle will be viewed in its many component parts. What is written speaks to the generalities of lifestyle since the various ethnic groups that comprise the population each have their own individual customs that represent their homeland. But the same would hold true in the United States, Canada or Australia, but to a lesser degree.

ARGENTINE CITIES: Argentina is essentially an urban country with regard to its total population. Most Argentinos live in cities or towns; however, many of the smaller towns are strictly agricultural or ranching service centers. Buenos Aires is the country's largest city, and its population alone accounts for 33 percent of the nation's population. When one considers the other major cities of Mendoza, Cordoba, Tucumán, Mar del Plata and Rosario, more than 60 percent of the population is accounted for. Argentine cities are similar to other Latin American cities only with regard to having a basic grid pattern that is focused upon the central plaza or in the case of Buenos Aires, several plaza areas around which are clustered the main church or cathedral and the local government buildings. But unlike the cities of other Latin American countries, there is a lack of the massive barrios, or slum areas that appear to infest the rest of the region, Chile, Uruguay and Costa Rica being the other exceptions. Yes there are poor barrios in Argentine cities, but they not only account for generally less than a fifth of the total area, but they are somewhat akin to poor neighborhoods in the other first world countries with regard to the overall quality of life, thus making them more livable than what would be found in other Latin American countries. One does not find square miles of tarpaper and wood shacks lacking basic utilities and lining dusty streets as would be seen in suburban Lima or Rio de Janeiro. This level of poverty simply is extremely limited in Argentina, and the extremely poor of this country are generally immigrants from the third would nations to the north of Argentina who have come seeking a better life. Also noted is the absence of the extensive use of barred windows, high walls and gates in the more upscale neighborhoods because there is no more domestic crime than would be found in the United States. Thus Argentine cities have a greater similarity to those of the United States or Canada with regard to their level of openness.

In all Argentine cities, the downtown or "centro" is the heart of the city. Urban decay is not found to be the problem that it is in the United States. The urban centers are vibrant and contain retail shopping, restaurants, nightclubs and a variety of office buildings and hotels that serve as the true hub of the city. Architecturally speaking, these downtown areas possess much late 19th and early 20th century architecture that is more reminiscent of Europe, especially that of France or Spain, giving them a distinctive flavor unlike anything else in Latin America.

In the larger cities, especially in Buenos Aires, there are some suburban shopping centers, but the dominance of the large mall concept has yet to take hold in Argentina's urban landscape. Each residential neighborhood possesses localized shopping, and of course super markets do exist, but the majority of shops are small, family-owned and cater to the needs of people living in the immediate vicinity. There is a great variety of merchandise available, and Argentine people are great consumers, at least those who can afford to be, which is a large percentage of the population. There is great abundance in the category of food because of the fact that Argentina produces far more than its population is capable of consuming.

Apart from Buenos Aires, Argentine cities are not bisected by freeways, cutting off one section of the city from another. Only Buenos Aires exhibits a degree of freeway development. In contrast to the lack of urban freeway networks, all Argentine cities are well endowed with public transportation, primarily in the form of busses. However, Buenos Aires, being such a massive city, does possess a very modern subway system locally known as the SubT along with commuter rail services.

All Argentine cities possess extensive park areas, a similarity to cities in Europe as opposed to the rest of Latin America. Parks range in size from the large, monumental grounds that surround public buildings or serve as the city's showpiece to small neighborhood plazas. Likewise, public buildings in Argentina are ornate and possess that European style of elegance, most dating to the 18th and 19th centuries. These buildings include museums, government offices, railway stations and exhibition halls, all heavily ornamented in a manner more akin to that of France, as the people of Argentina never strayed far from their Old World roots.

As will later be explored, Buenos Aires is a massive city that is totally out of proportion to all other cities in Argentina. It is considered to be a world-class city not only in its size, but also with regard to its lifestyle and sophistication. It is often referred to as the "Paris of the Americas." The other cities of Argentina pale by comparison, the largest having only around 1,000,000 people in contrast to the more than 15,200,000 that live in the capital. The second largest city is Rosario with only 1,200,000 residents. Throughout most of South America, the concept of one major city in each country, generally the capital is commonplace with the exception of Brazil because of its massive population and physical size. When one looks at the map of Argentina, it is plain to see how the railroad lines and highways radiate outward from Buenos Aires like spokes on a wheel. This one city is truly the hub of the nation.

HOME LIFE AND FAMILY: The people of Argentina are generally very family oriented. This stems from a combination of the strong family bonds that are typical to Spanish culture as well as to the various ethnic groups that have settled in the country. Argentine people are proud of their family traditions, and family gatherings are still events to be savored. Generations maintain close ties, and it is not uncommon among more traditional families for young members to engage in dating at a much later age than in the United States, Canada or Australia. Until recently, many traditional families still sent along the "dueña" or chaperone when young people dated. Older family members are more likely to live at home with their children and grandchildren if they are unable to take care of themselves, the idea of the nursing home or retirement center still being essentially foreign.

Like in so much of Europe, social life within the family revolves around food. Argentine people love to eat and drink, and the dinner table is often the primary social gathering spot. Dinner is the important meal of the day, but it is served much later than in North America. Dinner is often eaten at 9 PM, and people linger over the table for several hours.

Upscale Argentine homes are not that different from those in other first world nations, middle and upper class families having all of the modern conveniences we are accustomed to. However, in all Argentine homes, there is a distinct dining room, separate from the formal living room, and both are generally furnished with a decidedly European flair.

There are still major distinctions between rich and poor, but not to the degree found in other Latin American countries. However, in defense of Latin American tradition, the rich in Argentina do live lavish lifestyles. Architecturally, Argentine homes are very similar in style to those found in Spain; older neighborhoods showing faceless facades to the street, with the home encircling an interior patio. Most suburban housing is more akin to that found in North America, but stucco is the predominant building material. In urban areas, there is a strong emphasis upon apartment and condominium living with many of the older buildings showing a distinct French style of ornate architecture. Modern high-rise, however, are similar to those of all world urban centers. Suburban housing would not be unlike that in the United States or Canada, with homes having front and back yards, often unfenced, a contrast to much of the rest of Latin America where walls often enclose more affluent homes because of the great disparities in income and high residential crime rates.

FOOD AND MUSIC: The food and music of any country tell one a lot about how the people live. And these two aspects of lifestyle reflect so much of the spirit of the country. In Argentina, meat is king. This is one of the world's major beef producing nations, with its large estancias raising tremendous herds of cattle. Eating beef is a tradition that dates back to colonial times when there was not much in the way of imports, and people relied upon what the land could produce. The "asado" is an Argentine tradition that permeates every aspect of dining. At home, people grill meat in fire pits either inside or outdoors, and in restaurants, large fire pits are used to grill beef, lamb and chicken, but in large quantities. A typical meal would begin with various salads, often including native vegetables such as the heart of the yucca root. This will be followed by the main course consisting of various types of grilled meats and sausages, accompanied by potatoes or rice. Desserts in Argentina are very European, including the traditional flan, but also expressed in a variety of elegant pastries.

Strong coffee is popular, especially at breakfast. Most Argentinos eat a rather light breakfast of fruit, croissants or rolls, a bit of cheese and washed down by coffee. Lunch is often also a light meal, the traditional empanada being the most popular item. An empanada is a flaky pastry wrapped around meat or chicken, often topped with an avocado sauce similar to guacamole. The popular drink during the day is a native brew called yerba mate. The mate leaves are placed in a small gourd like container, often made of silver, and then allowed to steep. It is drunk through a small straw made out of the same material as the gourd-like container. It is very bitter, but the Argentine people claim that it has healthful properties. No doubt today's scientists would consider it to be high in anti oxidants, similar to tea.

The people of Argentina have a great love for music. There is a strong beat to the traditional Argentine folk music that reaches one's soul. The pulsating beat, often produced by simply slapping the side of the guitar, accompanies the strumming of the strings while the singer's voice rises and falls in what could almost be called a wail. There are strong southern Spanish influences, some would say even Moorish, in the music of Argentina. It is haunting and a part of the national character that is very moving. Likewise in dance, the Spanish flamenco influence can be seen, but in Argentina it led to a very sensuous dance that was later exported to the entire world and known as tango. Argentine people are almost addicted to tango, and in large cities such as Buenos Aires, there are special nightclubs where people go to either dance or simply watch. Some say that tango originated in the dock area of Buenos Aires, and no doubt there is truth to this. But it is deeply rooted in the traditional folk music much of which came from the large estancias on The Pampas.

In rural areas, people love to gather and listen to folk songs, often accompanied by one or more guitars. The songs are often about the land, or about the usual themes of love. And in many local neighborhood restaurants in the cities, people also gather to either listen or join in to the singing of popular folk songs.

URBAN SOPHISTICATION VS. RURAL SIMPLICITY: As noted previously, the general cultural flavor of Argentina has a strong European theme running through it. This is primarily the result of the cultural matrix exhibiting heavy European immigration combined with the fact that the Argentine nation always prided itself in its Spanish roots. Nowhere is the flavor of Europe as strong as in the cities. There is a level of sophistication among wealthy Argentine people that is heavily French or Italian when it comes to the pleasures of life. Sidewalk cafes, small bistros and boutiques dominate the central shopping districts, and the people still believe in dressing up. Clothing and high fashion are paramount to the upper class of Argentina, especially in Buenos Aires. Among the middle and lower income people, fine clothes are also important for special events such as baptisms, marriages and holidays.

One of the most unique of Argentine customs is that of placing emphasis upon the human body as an element of beauty. Nowhere in the modern world does the national health scheme support cosmetic surgery for sheer vanity. In Argentina there is a passion for cosmetic surgery simply for the purpose of improving upon what nature has given a person. From the rural farmer to the elite city dweller, all can have nose or ear bobs; tummy tucks or face lifts at government expense simply to improve personal appearance. Some Argentinos carry it to the extreme, especially as they reach upper middle age.

In the vast ranch lands of the Pampas and Patagonia, the Argentine gaucho, or what we could call cowboy, is still a part of the less sophisticated rural scene. These rugged ranch hands do not live the same lives as their ancestors, but they still maintain many of the traditions of those who came before. Ranch hands are important on the large estancias, but modern tools augment their lives rather than that of the gaucho of the 19th century. Like in the United States and Australia, there is much lore and legend surrounding these cowboys. And in both their everyday work and for fiestas, the gauchos can be seen in traditional dress, which is quite unlike that of an American or Australian cowboy and more like that of a Spanish rancher.

In many rural communities, especially along the foothills of the Andes and in Patagonia, there are enclaves of specific immigrant cultures that still maintain their traditional lifestyle patterns. Communities of Welsh, German or Italian families adhere to the traditions of the mother country, these being reflected in everyday life. For example, in Bariloche it is possible to be served a traditional British tea in the afternoon, or have a good German strudel in one of the city's many cafes.

ARGENTINE TRANSPORTATION SERVICES: Argentina is a large country, and transportation is key to the success of such a nation where distance factors into the economic equation. With the political climate changing so often in past years, the Argentine economy has seen its rise and fall, and as a result, some of its transport infrastructure has suffered.

Argentina possesses the most extensive railroad network of any country in South America. Buenos Aires is of course the hub of the entire system. As the country's greatest seaport, all railway lines funneled goods into and out of Buenos Aires. Today the railroad still plays a major role with regard to the carrying of freight, but it has suffered greatly when it comes to passenger services. Apart from commuter rail services serving the immediate suburban sprawl of Buenos Aires, there are few passenger trains connecting the capital with the rest of the country. The only services to still exist are those in the heartland of the country, connecting the cities and towns of the Pampas with Buenos Aires, and they are not always reliable.

In contrast to the limited nature of passenger rail service, the country still maintains viable air services, connecting the major cities of the country as well as providing links between Argentina and nations across South America and abroad. The national airline is Aerolineas Argentinas. It connects Buenos Aires with several major cities in the United States, Europe and Australia, but of course it must compete with two major foreign carriers that have also been granted the right to serve Argentina. The travel time between Los Angeles and Buenos Aires is approximately 12 hours, while from New York the travel time is around 10 hours. Travel time to Europe averages 12 to 14 hours. Remember that Argentina is in the Southern Hemisphere, and a look at the globe will show you that the distance from the Pacific Coast of the United States is actually greater than that from the Atlantic Coast since South America is actually farther east than North America with regard to longitude.

Argentina maintains an extensive highway network, especially in the Pampas and along the central Andean foothills. The country does not possess a significant motorway network, as the Argentine people do not take to the road in the manner that North Americans or Europeans do. Most of Argentina's highways are well paved, but only two lanes wide, often narrow in the more remote areas. However, between the major cities of the Pampas and the central Andes, the roads are relatively wide and provide for easy accessibility. As one travels into the Gran Chaco or into Patagonia, there are fewer good paved roads, many being of gravel or dirt, but still easy to negotiate except during heavy rain or snow.

ARGENTINE SPORTS: The people of Argentina have a passion for soccer, known as futbol. Like many European nations, the people of Argentina revere their soccer stars, treating them with the same level of celebrity as we do our movie stars. Now retired soccer great Diego Maradona has been literally worshiped as a national idol. Many young Argentine children grow up dreaming of becoming a soccer idol. There are teams all over the country that vie for the national championships, with major matches held between February and July and again between August and December.

Horse racing is a major spectator sport, understandable in a country that has placed so much historic and economic emphasis upon the Pampas and the raising of horses and cattle. Going to the horse races is a major event, one that people still dress up for as they do in many European countries.

Tennis is a major game for personal enjoyment and as a spectator sport. Noted Argentine tennis stars that have been figures on the world stage are Gabriela Sabatini who reached the number three spot during 1991-93 and Guillermo Vilas who won 62 professional titles during his career, including three Gland Slams. In 1977, Villas was named tennis player of the year for having won 12 major titles, something that no other player has ever done.

Pato is a distinctly Argentinean sport, initially the game of the Gauchos on the Pampas. Two teams on horseback play it. The object of the game is to hold onto a duck in a leather pouch that has handles, which can be tightly gripped. The game is like a tug of war, and it became so dangerous that it was banned during the late 19th century. It was revived with new rules in the late 1930's. Today's pato is a leather ball with six handles that the teams attempt to throw into a goal basket at opposite ends of the field, sort of a cross between basketball and polo.

In recent years, the Argentine people have taken to volleyball, basketball, hockey and rugby. These sports are growing in popularity, especially as Argentine teams perform well in world championship matches.

In the ranching areas of the Pampas and Patagonia, local rodeos are still a popular sport, just as they are in Spain and México. But unlike their other Latin American counterparts, the Argentine people are not fond of bullfighting.

The people of Argentina also have a great love for the beach. However, many of those who live in the interior find a beach holiday to be a rare occasion, often necessitating traveling hundreds of miles. The great beach resorts are those on the Atlantic coast near Buenos Aires. As one proceeds farther south into Patagonia, the waters become colder as does the climate.

WINTER SPORTS: Argentina and Chile are the only two Latin American countries in which the general public has passionately accepted skiing, snowboarding and other winter sports. The southern reaches of the Andes near the city of Bariloche have become not only a favored summer holiday location, but they are now considered to be the best winter sports venue in all of South America. World-class ski resorts have developed, but as yet they do not hold great attraction for European or North American visitors. This is the result of the reversal of seasons. The prime winter season in Argentina is June through August, a period when most Northern Hemisphere winter sports enthusiasts have turned to other pursuits. However, those diehards have found that they can still enjoy winter sports if they are willing to travel to the southern reaches of Argentina, and each year there is a slow increase in North American or European skiers coming to either Argentina or Chile during the June-September period for the purpose of skiing.

Typical European architecture as seen in Buenos Aires

A bit of patriotic fervor with a street vendor in Buenos Aires

Buenos Aires does have extensive commuter rail service

North American open style of housing, seen here in Puerto Madryn

A barrio outside Puerto Madryn housing illegal Bolivian immigrants seeking a better way of life.

A strong Germanic influence in the architecture of Ushuaia

A pie made of dulce de leche is a popular Argentine dessert

Tango demonstrated in a small Patagonian town

LANDSCAPES OF CHILE

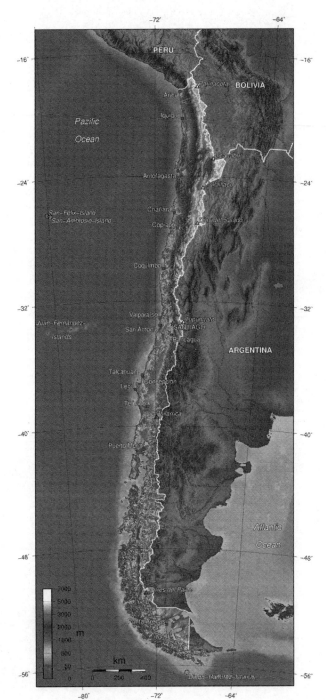

A locational map of major places in Chile (Work of Captain Blood, CCV BY SA 3.0, Wikimedia.org)

A location map of Chile showing the role of the Andes

Chile stands out among the countries of the world for its strange shape. No other nation comes anywhere close to approximating its unusual configuration. From its northern border with Peru to the tip of Cape Horn, Chile stretches over 4,297 kilometers or 2,670 miles. This is the same distance as from the city of Juneau, Alaska to the southern tip of the Baja California Peninsula. But what stands in sharp contrast to this extensive length is the narrow width of Chile. It averages 160 kilometers or 100 miles, with the widest portion of the country in the far northern deserts where it is 320 kilometers or 200 miles from the South Pacific Ocean to the border of Bolivia. In the far southern fjord region, there are places where the mainland portion of the country is only 50 miles wide, not counting the size of adjacent offshore islands. The total land area is only 756,950 square kilometers or 292,260 square miles, approximately the size of the American states of Texas and Oklahoma combined. The estimated 2015 population for Chile is 17,508,000 people, living primarily in the central valleys extending south into the lakes district.

What could account for a country developing such an absurdly long shape, essentially a ribbon of narrow land fronting on the ocean? The answer is simple, the Andes Mountains. The Andes, which begin in Venezuela and run as an unbroken mass of mountain clear to the southern tip of the continent, reach their ultimate height and impenetrability between Chile and Argentina. Mt. Aconcagua and Nevada Ojos del Salado are the highest and second highest mountains in the Western Hemisphere and among the ten tallest mountains on earth, rising to elevations in excess of 6,705 meters or 22,000 feet. There are very few passes through the mountains, and those that do exist are snowbound the entire winter, thus preventing easy communication. So the Spanish who colonized west of the Andes could only expand their colonial settlements to the north and south along the base of the mountains, while the Spanish who settled east of the Andes could also only spread north and south, but occupying a far greater mass of land that became Argentina. The Argentine nation is not quite as long as Chile, but it also extends for over 3,200 kilometers or 2,000 miles, but at its widest point, it is over 700 miles from border to border.

From a geological perspective, Chile is an unstable and fragile country. The nation sits along the border of the South American Plate. The Nazca Plate in the north and the Antarctic plate in the south are pushing eastward and driving down under the South American Plate. As a result, there is a deep trench off the coast, but unseen to observers. Essentially Chile sits at the edge of a great escarpment, at its deepest point it is over 7,315 meters or 24,000 feet in depth. The movement of the plate causes what is called subduction. The result is a string of volcanic peaks interspersed through the Andes, many of them active from time to time. In addition, the entire region is subjected to earthquakes, which can be catastrophic. In 1960, the movement of the Nazca Plate caused a magnitude 9.5 earthquake, the largest ever recorded on the Richter scale. One portion of coastline was offset by over 30 feet for a length of over 700 miles. Fortunately Chile is a prosperous country and its buildings are for the most part well constructed. Although there was widespread destruction, the amount of devastation and the loss of life were far less than what would have occurred had Chile been a third world nation. During the 20th century, 28 major earthquakes each with a Richter scale magnitude of over 6.9 hit Chile. Essentially this is greater activity than seen in California or Alaska, but the geological principals are the same as those of the Pacific Northwest coast. In 2011 there were two magnitude 7.1 earthquakes in south central Chile. The last two major earthquake took place in April 2014 in northern Chile and had a magnitude of 8.2 on the Richter scale and more recently a magnitude 8.3 occurred in northern Chile in September 2015.

It is the tectonic and volcanic activity created by plate movement that created the Andes Mountains and gave Chile its incredible backdrop. The Andes are essentially a young range of mountains, still continuing to develop. Part of that growth is through vulcanism, and during the 20th century, nearly 60 of the more than 600 volcanoes in this region saw periods of eruption. The newest volcano to be formed is Navidad Volcano in southern Chile, which developed its cone in a matter of weeks, having first erupted on Christmas day 1988. In April 2015, there was a massive eruption of Calbuco Volcano, a snow covered peak that is located in the southern Lake District very close to the city of Puerto Montt. It did damage several small villages, but the major Lake District towns and Puerto Montt were spared.

Over 80 percent of the total land surface of Chile is classed as either mountainous or hilly. This leaves very little land for development, but fortunately the population being relatively small, Chile is far from being considered overcrowded. The Andes form the backdrop for the entire country, running the full length of Chile. They are spectacular, especially when viewed from the lowland valleys, presenting a wall of mountain that stretches from horizon to horizon, capped in snow for a minimum half of the year, with the higher peaks being permanently draped in white. The coastal mountains, often called the Precordillera, are much lower. In the north, they extend westward from the Andes, sheltering valleys in their midst. Farther south, they run parallel to the coast, sheltering a central valley similar in nature to California, home to the core of the nation's population. In the far south, the coastal mountains have been dissected by glacial action, the river valleys forming deep-water fjords and breaking the land into islands, as rising sea level flooded between the higher peaks. This region is often difficult to navigate because of the multitude of small islands and narrow channels, but it is a spectacular region with great scenic potential. Roads are few because of the difficulty of construction due to the interruption of the land surface by deep water fjords. It is often necessary to cross into Argentina to continue the journey south to the Straits of Magellan.

Chile possesses one of the world's longest coastlines, but much of it is rather formidable. High cliffs or mountains border most of the coastline. This allows the surf to pound against the shore with spectacular results. There are some sheltered beaches in the northern and central reaches, but in the south, the mountains appear to slide directly into the ocean, producing numerous bays, channels and fjords similar to that of the coastline of Alaska and Norway. All along the coast, the Humboldt Current washes Chile with rather cold water. Only at latitude 45 degrees south does the South Pacific Current bring warm water over the top of the cold Humboldt Current, providing the necessary fuel for the precipitation that falls in the southern one third of the country mainly as snow.

Chile can be viewed within the framework of climatic regions, as there are three different landscapes within this long, narrow country. Each is distinctive, and where one meets the other, there is obviously a transition zone as the northern deserts grade into the mild Mediterranean center, which in turn slowly merges with the maritime cooler climate of the far south. The remainder of this chapter will look at each of these three regions.

THE ATACAMA DESERT: Northern Chile presents one of the world's driest landscapes. In this part of the country, the cold waters of the Humboldt Current wash the shores while during most of the year a sub tropical high-pressure ridge remains over the water. The combination of descending air out of the high traversing cold water inhibits the necessary convection to create rainfall. The land remains dry year around, only on occasion experiencing rain showers, especially during years when the El Niño condition alters the normal patterns.

There are stations along the Chileno coast that can go for decades without reporting any measurable precipitation. So the question arises as to how vegetation can survive. Small scrubby plants have developed the means whereby their leaves can extract evening dew that forms as maritime air drifts across the shoreline. The fast flowing streams that run down from the Andean slopes also provide sustenance for limited tree growth along their course. But essentially the Atacama Desert is one of the driest zones on earth, a landscape that for all intents is hostile, bleak, yet captivating in its starkness. People have lived in the region for thousands of years, and the Spanish settlers discovered that they could survive and prosper by locating their settlements adjacent to one of the Andean rivers or streams that supplied fresh water year around.

The landscape of the Atacama Desert consists of an alternation of transverse mountains that run east to west, intermingled with basins that are often filled with salt flats resulting from small streams that loose themselves before reaching the sea. The desert is one of rocky pavement and there are few dunes, as one might expect under conditions of such aridity. To the east, the Andean foothills remain equally as bleak at elevations up to 10,000 feet, ultimately stepping up into the high plateau or Altiplano once one crosses the Bolivian border. The higher peaks, many of them active volcanic cones, are draped in snow, providing for a stark contrast with the lowland deserts. This is a landscape of brown soil, white snowcaps and deep blue skies. Adding to this surreal environment, there are small brackish lakes, each with a salt encrusted shoreline as well as fields of geothermal hot springs and geysers, lending an even more hostile look to the region. Yet there are scattered shrubs and grasses able to survive under these conditions, feeding small numbers of the South American llama and limited bird life.

THE CENTRAL VALLEY REGION: The heartland of Chile is the central valley region, home to the bulk of the nation's population. At approximately 30 degrees south latitude, the transverse mountains of the Atacama Desert give way to ranges of low mountains that parallel the coast, separated from the Andes Mountains by a narrow valley that extends 895 kilometers or 500 miles in length to where is truncated by the Golfo Corcovado, a large fjord resulting from glacial action. The central valley region is not perfectly flat like the great Central Valley of California. It is rather a series of interconnecting valleys often separated by low intervening hills. The climate of this region represents a transition zone. During summer, the sub tropical high pressure, which moves slightly south, bringing dry, stable conditions. In winter, the high-pressure ridge retreats northward to the Atacama Desert. This allows the prevailing westerly winds to sweep in off the South Pacific Ocean, brining blustery rainstorms that result from the interplay of the South Pacific and Humboldt Currents. This type of climatic pattern is referred to as Mediterranean. It is a prized climate found outside of the Mediterranean Basin in central California, the southwestern tip of Africa, the southwestern and south central portions of Australia and here in central Chile. The mix of dry summer and mild, wet winter is ideal for settlement, and it is especially favorable for a mixed agriculture that enables the raising of a broad variety of crops, especially table vegetables, stone fruits and vines. With its strong European cultural tradition, especially Spanish and Italian, Chile has become one of the world's major producers of high quality wines.

One drawback to the topographic configuration of the central valley region is the formation of summer inversion layers that trap atmospheric pollutants from urban centers. Like California, this region suffers from bouts of smog, especially in and around the major city of Santiago.

The vegetation of the central valley region consists of a mix of scrub woodland, both broadleaf evergreen and deciduous species combined with larger canopy trees along watercourses. As you proceed into the Andean foothills, the vegetation thickens into chaparral type woodland, as is seen in the world's other Mediterranean regions. Many European species have also been planted around farms and ranches as well as in the urban centers. On the drier northern side of the region there are even species of cacti that are closely related to the saguaro of the Sonoran Desert in Arizona. Similar species are also found in northern Argentina on the leeward lower slopes of the Andes.

The coastline of the central valley region is primarily rugged, with hills descending to the ocean in a series of cliffs. However, there are sections where sandy beaches do occur naturally, and these are well used by the population of the region. Although the ocean current is a cold one, with warm summer days in the upper 20's Celsius or 80's Fahrenheit to even low 30's Celsius or 90's Fahrenheit, water temperatures in the upper teens Celsius or 50's and low 60's are braved. Chilenos show the same stoic qualities, as do Californians when it comes to utilizing their shoreline for recreational purposes.

SOUTHERN CHILE: If it were not for the differences in vegetation, someone from Alaska or British Columbia visiting southern Chile would believe that he is at home. This is a spectacular region of tall mountain crags that have experienced glacial scour combined with individual volcanic cones of significant proportion. Heavy snowfields and active glaciers give the mountains a level of magnificence while at the same time making them rather formidable barrier when it comes to connecting Chile with Argentina. To further hinder the use of these southern lands, every river valley descending from the Andes to the South Pacific Ocean experienced glacial action, thus their lower reaches were scoured below present sea level. As the waters rose with the last glacial melt, these lowlands were flooded. In some areas, whole ranges of mountain were cut off from the mainland to stand as offshore islands. Seawater flooded deep into many valleys, in some instances well into the higher foothills, creating fjords, ocean channels that are essentially miles inland from the open sea, and protected by the offshore islands.

The overall climate of southern Chile is classified as maritime or marine west coast. This results from the interplay of warm and cold ocean currents, which produce intense winter storm cells that are then driven on shore by the prevailing westerly winds. As the unstable air is forced to rise by the mountains, prolonged periods of warm front rain occur along the coast while snow falls in prodigious amounts in the higher country. Summers are somewhat drier, but still relatively cool and overall still moist. As a result, there is a high percentage of cloud cover, marine fog or mist and this is conducive to the luxuriant growth of vegetation.

The native evergreen and deciduous trees thrive in this climate, producing lush forests often underlain by ferns and wildflowers. The most common trees in the best-watered regions are the southern beech, which is a broadleaf deciduous and the araucaria, a primitive ancestor of modern conifers. One of the most magnificent trees, also a primitive ancestor to Northern Hemisphere conifers is the Fitz-roya cupressoides, growing to considerable heights, but only in isolated coastal pockets. In the lower Andean reaches, there are also many species of broadleaf evergreen trees, thus producing an exceptionally diverse forest landscape when viewed from lowest to highest elevations. On leeward slopes that do not catch as much rainfall, there are areas of open grassland or "puna," often bleak and windswept.

Alpaca and vicuña graze on the drier slopes of the Andes, especially on the more leeward margins. These rather elusive relatives of the llama are prized for their wool, and native people considered them to be sacred. They are difficult to grow commercially, but some ranchers in the southern margins of Chile and Argentina have managed to breed them successfully in captivity.

The northern reaches of the region gently blend into the central valley region. As you travel south, temperatures become cooler and there is more annual rainfall. The central valley region dries out during the summer while to the south the land remains green. By the time you reach Valdivia, the maritime environment dominates. At Puerto Montt the coastline swings east, closer to the Andes, truncating the continuous stretches of land that contain valleys that began at the border of Peru. From here south, there is very limited level land, as glacial action and later coastal flooding reduced lowlands to a minimum. Essentially Puerto Montt is land's end for road traffic. To connect the remainder of southern Chile to the rest of the nation, boat and air traffic take over. This is virtually the same situation as found in Alaska and British Columbia, and to some degree in northern Norway.

The region around Valdivia and Puerto Montt is one that is also dotted with many glacial lakes. The combination of fresh water lakes, fast flowing streams, thick forests and a backdrop of majestic volcanoes makes this one of the most popular regions of Chile as will later be discussed. This region corresponds with the lake district of Bariloche in Argentina, which is on the opposite side of the Andes in the same latitudinal range.

The mainland of South America comes to an end at the Straits of Magellan, separating the continent from the large offshore island of Tierra del Fuego, shared by both Chile and Argentina. Tierra del Fuego is actually part of the continent, but glacial scour on both sides of the continental divide combined with plate tectonic action created the straits, a water connection between oceans. From a commercial perspective the straits provide a sheltered route for major ships to pass between the Atlantic and Pacific Oceans where these ships are too large to transit the Panama Canal. Thus a significant amount of traffic still traverses these most southerly waters.

The continent technically ends with a small island off the southern tip of Tierra del Fuego. It is here that a jutting headland known as Cape Horn is land's end. But much of the year the waters are very stormy, thus ships use the Straits of Magellan rather than venturing around Cape Horn.

ISLA DE PASCUA and ISLAS JUAN FERNÁNDEZ: There is a Chileno colony located over 3,200 kilometers or 2,000 miles west in the South Pacific Ocean that is one of the most unique of territories. It lies just below the Tropic of Capricorn, yet it is a barren land, cloaked only in grass and a few shrubs. The translation of the name should help in better understanding Easter Island. It was here that a Polynesian people settled over 1,000 years ago. As a part of their religion and mythology, they built massive stone monoliths, utilizing the timber of the island in their need to roll these giant statues down to the coastal margins of the island. Ultimately war must have destroyed the culture once the ecosystem was ruined. Although not a mainland portion of the country, no discussion of Chile can be complete without mention of this island, which is essentially a large volcanic mound that is truly a part of the realm of Oceania.

About 360 miles west of the central Chileno coast are the small islands of Juan Fernández. The islands are of volcanic origin and are very rocky with limited anchorage. The Spanish first discovered them in 1574, and over the centuries the British and French attempted to gain their possession for strategic purposes. The islands are today protected as a national park; their vegetation is slowly being restored since early Spanish settlers brought goats as part of their settlement, nearly ruining the vegetation. One of the islands known as Isla de Robinson Caruso, is so named as the author Daniel Defoe used this island as the setting for his famous novel about being stranded.

The winter landscape of the Atacama Desert of northern Chile (Work of M M from Switzerland, CC BY SA 2.0, Wikimedia.org)

The Atacama meets the volcanoes of the Andes (Work of Daniel Nussbaum, CC BY SA 3.0, Wikimedia.org)

The richness of agriculture in the Central Valley

The Carretera Internacional connecting Chile to Argentina through the Andes

Climbing the switchbacks to the Argentine border - a driving challenge

The high mountain ski resort of Valle Nevado above Santiago

In the Lake District of southern Chile, looking at Osorno Volcano

Maca Volcano towers above the inside passage south of Puerto Montt

Magnificent Aisén Fjord in southern Chile

The San Rafael Glacier - largest in Chile

The Beagle Channel along the shore of Tierra del Fuego

The face of Glacier Garibaldi tucked into a small fjord on Tierra del Fuego

CHILENO HISTORY/GOVERNMENT

Looking into the history of Chile enables you to understand how this country with its strange elongated shape came into being. Given the mountain barrier presented by the Andes, there is no way such a vast, elongated land with different climatic zones could have ever been unified with Argentina, nor could it have ever been controlled from the north out of Peru. Thus the logical course was for a colony to develop in the most favorable of regions, which happened to be the central valley area, and then spread its influence up and down the coast, constantly hemmed in by the mountain barrier.

Prior to the coming of the Spanish, Chile was controlled by two distinct native tribes. The Quechua, the most powerful of these people being those who established the Inca Empire, occupied the northern deserts. Parts of the Atacama Desert fell under Inca control, as there were valuable mineral deposits that added wealth to the nation. The Araucanian tribes occupied the central portion of Chile and their settlement extended into the northern portions of the fjord country of the south. These were a fierce people who did not welcome Spanish intrusion, and this ultimately led to their destruction.

The first European known to have visited Chile was Ferdinand Magellan; the Portuguese explorer who's around the world voyage gave a true measure to the size of South America. In 1520, his ship sailed through the straits that now bear his name and he landed briefly on one of the southern islands. But the expedition did not lay any claims to the land. After Pizarro's conquest of the Inca Empire in 1535, one of his officers led an expedition that made its way into northern Chile, but again no attempt at settlement was made. Spanish colonists finally settled the central valley region when Pedro de Valdivia, one of Pizarro's generals, established Santiago in 1541. Concepcion was settled in 1550 and Valdivia was established in 1552. The Spanish found the central valley to be so much like the interior and southern coastal regions of Spain that it was easy to build a new colony here, however the Araucanians harassed them until the latter portion of the 19th century, just as the Apache hindered settlement in the American Southwest for as long a time.

The colony in central Chile prospered, despite ongoing warfare with the natives. By the middle of the 17th century, the population had reached 100,000 and by the middle of the 18th century it was 500,000. In the middle of the 19th century, Chile had over 1,000,000 people, but they were concentrated primarily in the central region between Santiago and Concepcion. And in the late 19th century copper discoveries in the north brought workers out of the center to the forbidding Atacama Desert. At the same time, immigration from central and northern Europe brought in people accustomed to and actually in favor of living in cooler more moist climates. These immigrants, primarily Germanic, settled in southern Chile, where to this day their cultural influence is far heavier than that of the Spanish.

During its period of colonization, Chile was a part of the Viceroyalty of Peru, administered from Lima, communication normally maintained by sea since the land journey was long and parched. Initially no valuable minerals were discovered and the people made their living by supplying Lima and the Peruvian mines with vital foodstuffs, thus there were few enticements for Peruvians to settle that far from the Viceroyalty's capital. Southern Chile remained in the hand of the Araucanians until they were ultimately defeated in the mid 19th century. It was only then that European immigrants could safely settle the lands to the south. The Chileno people resented the domination of Spanish rule exerted from far off Peru. In 1810 they declared their independence on September 18th, but freedom did not come easily. Large landowners of European origin controlled the country, and it was difficult for them to agree upon a system of government or its leadership. The instability that followed the independence declaration caused the country to remain weak and its government ineffective. Ultimately the Spanish military was able to re capture the central region and in 1814, Chile was once again under Spanish rule. But it was at this same time that Argentina, under the strong influence of General José de San Martin, was gaining its independence. A Chileno dissident, General Bernardo O'Higgins ultimately led his forces, along with those sent by General San Martin to force the Spanish to concede. In 1818, Chile was won its independence and O'Higgins became the country's first president, but the last of Spanish royalist forces were not defeated in southern Chile until 1826. The name of O'Higgins alone shows that the European mix in Chile was broad, not just Spanish as was true in so many Latin American countries to the north.

As president, O'Higgins ruled with a firm hand, some of today's historians refer to him as a dictator. He worked to improve the country's infrastructure by building schools, developing a road network, establishing public health programs and clamping down on bandits who roamed the countryside. He also attempted to build up foreign trade. He ultimately faced strong opposition from the upper class who truly ran the country's economy, and in 1823 he resigned. But he is recognized today as the country's liberator, and there are statues of him to be found in most major cities.

Under a liberally written constitution, Chile experienced strife between the conservative landed gentry and the populace at large until 1830 when General Joaquín Prieto seized control of the government and became president. His administration ultimately wrote a new constitution in 1833 that vested immense powers in the executive branch of government as well as giving almost all power to the central government and very little to regional authority. Liberal factions attempted to overthrow the conservative majority by force in 1835, 1851 and 1859, but were unsuccessful. Although the Conservative Party did not have full support of the general populace, they did promote the development of a healthy agricultural economy, the building of the first railroads and development of mineral resources. The liberal wing of the Conservative Party joined in coalition with the Liberal Party and was able to force through many social reforms during the early 1860's and this diffused many of the tensions that had led to near overthrow of the government.

The conservative government also initiated conflicts with neighboring countries, the first being with Peru and Bolivia over the Atacama Desert where vast deposits of nitrate and copper were found. The nitrate was considered a valuable commodity because of its use to make smokeless gunpowder. During the period of 1879 to 1883, Chile expanded its influence north into the Atacama Desert. The dispute over a vague border brought Chile into conflict with Peru and Bolivia because all three nations claimed possession of the same territory where nitrate, used in the manufacture of smokeless powder, existed in large quantities. What became known as the War of the Pacific ended as the Chileno army prevailed. The Treaty of Ancon in 1884 ceded the Atacama to Chile from Peru. In addition, Bolivia's narrow section of Atacama territory was also lost. Not only did the winning of this war bring the entire north into Chileno possession, but also it forever severed Bolivia's outlet to the sea, making it one of only two landlocked nations in South America. However, today's ties with Bolivia are close and the Bolivianos can export freely through northern Chileno ports.

Chile saw its first and only major revolution of the 19th century in 1881 when forces allied to the Roman Catholic Church revolted against Presidente José Manuel Balmaceda. Navy Captain Jorge Montt led a group of fellow officers, known as Congresionalists, against the Chileno fleet in the north, seizing the nitrate rich lands. Ultimately they defeated the army, capturing Valparaiso and Santiago. Although a short war, nearly 10,000 people died and much property was destroyed. This revolt brought down the Balmaceda government, as the President committed suicide and Montt became president. Montt managed to pacify both liberal and conservative elements in the country and was able to build on the nation's economic potential. He extended political reforms that resulted in more actual participation in government by the ordinary Chilenos, but this ultimately led to more political unrest and turbulence, but no further violent revolutions.

Given the geology of Chile, natural disasters are to be expected. During the country's founding years there were few major earthquakes or volcanic eruptions in areas that were heavily populated. But in August 1906, that changed when a catastrophic earthquake struck Valparaiso and Santiago. The death toll was over 3,000 with more than 100,000 people made homeless. Had it not been for relatively good construction techniques, the death toll would have been much higher. This would not be the last major catastrophic quake to hit the country, a topic that will again re surface in this historic chapter.

Chile entered the 20th century in relative peace and with economic stability. During World War I, the country remained neutral, as did much of South America. In the post war period, however, as economic prosperity continued to increase, the country dove into political turmoil. Again it was the conflict between Conservative and Liberal Party ideals. The Liberal Party managed to win the 1920 election and Arturo Alessandri Palma became president, but he was unsuccessful in achieving any of the reforms his party had hoped for. In 1924, the age-old problem of Latin America reared its head in Chile – a military coup d'état. Remember Argentina and all of their coups. Alessandri was forced out of office, but the military surprisingly forced through his liberal reforms, but in the process established a dictatorship, which was overthrown in 1925 by still another military coup. This coup restored Alessandri to power and saw to the writing of a new constitution that reformed the electoral process, strengthened the executive branch and defined the relationship between the Roman Catholic Church and the government. However, Alessandri's term lasted less than one year,

Stability at last came to Chile when army officer Carlos Ibáñez came to power in 1927 and ruled until 1931. A period of short-lived coups again threw the country into turmoil until the 1932 election when Alessandri once again won the election, this time serving his full six-year term, retiring in 1938. In the next election, a very liberal government was elected as a coalition between various democratic groups, placing Pedro Aguirre Cerda as president. He set about to establish new economic reforms, but the country was once again hit by a severe 8.3 magnitude earthquake in 1939, killing nearly 30,000 people. Despite this severe interruption to the coalition's plans, they won re election in 1942. However, World War II brought divisions with the Chileno government as many people with Germanic ancestry favored the country siding with the Axis powers. Presidente Ríos managed to maintain a pro Allied position and Chile officially declared war on Axis powers in 1944, but saw no major action by its forces. Following the war, the country became one of the charter members of the United Nations in 1945.

An outgrowth of the war years was a rise of membership in the Communist Party, given that many Chilenos are of central European background, favoring very liberal political leanings. This left leaning tendency would ultimately lead the country to a major showdown between left and right whose ramifications rippled all the way back to the United States. In 1946, Gabriel Gonzáez Videla, leader of the Radical Party won the election supported by the Communist Party. As a show of appreciation, he appointed three Communist Party members to his cabinet. The coalition broke apart in six months because the Radical and Communist Party ideologies clashed. The Radical Party turned on the Communists, severing relations with the Soviet Union in 1947, arrested hundreds of Communist Party members under a draconian law known as the Law for the Defense of Democracy. The same law also outlawed the Communist Party, a move that the United States applauded.

The next few years saw literal chaos come to Chile. The country's labor movement was strongly socialistic and many had supported the Communist Party. Former President Ibáñez led a military revolt that was quickly crushed, but turmoil continued to mount. In a complete turn around to the actions of the Radical Party, the next election saw General Ibáñez win by means of the ballot box. But he was essentially only effective in restoring some order to the country. The economic and social problems that grew out of so much unrest only continued to plague the country's ability to function.

In the 1958 election, the son of former president Arturo Alessandri Palma, Jorge Alessandri Rodríguez was elected president, this time as a compromise coalition of both the Conservative and Liberal Party. The once again legal Communist Party opposed Rodríguez, and the new Christian Democratic Party, but his coalition's promise of tax reform, agrarian reform and massive building projects appealed to the people. The government strengthened its ties to the United States and broke its relations with Cuba, but also resumed ties with the Soviet Union.

Chile was once again struck by natural disaster, which dampened the government's plans for new development. In 1960, a magnitude 9.5 earthquake rocked southern Chile, touching off both tsunami and volcanic eruptions. The massive quake, which lasted nearly seven minutes, was followed by violent aftershocks of such intensity that the geological community marks this event as the most catastrophic in modern history. Fortunately once again, Chile's sound architecture kept the death toll amazingly low for such a violent episode. Throughout the history of Chile, devastating earthquakes have been a fact of life due to the country's proximity to the massive undersea subduction zone. The future holds more such calamities in store for this nation.

The next election in 1964 brought the Christian Democratic Party to power, but the new government's partial nationalization of the copper industry angered both the left and right, causing massive public demonstration. By the 1970 election, Chilenos were ready for major changes, and that is what they received. The leftist opposition formed a new Popular Unity coalition that brought Salvador Allende Gossens to power. His platform was one of pure socialism including nationalization of industries, banks and communications. With only 37 percent of the votes, the Congress declared his party the winner and Allende became the first Marxist-Leninist leaning president to be elected in the Americas, an event that made the United States exceptionally uneasy.

Allende wasted no time in turning the country into a socialist nation by instituting all of the state controls over the economy, banking and communications just as he had promised. He also imposed strict measures on the accumulation of capital and raised worker's wages in an attempt to gain their support. His actions only served to divide the nation. And economically his programs proved disastrous, as inflation went out of control and political violence erupted to a level not seen before in the 20th century. On September 11, 1973, military leaders seized power in another coup d'état. Fearing for his life as a military captive, Allende committed suicide, but to this day many in both Chile and the United States claim that the CIA assassinated him. The United States has denied the allegations, but the louder America protested the more widespread the belief to this day in both countries. The United States feared the creation of another Cuba even though Allende was not a true Communist.

Many Chilenos were at first relieved to have the military back in power and the socialism of Allende undone. But their hopes were soon dashed when the military junta leader General Augusto Pinochet Ugarte began to exhibit dictatorial powers. He suspended the constitution, disbanded the Congress, dissolved all political parties and imposed strict censorship on the media. His police state policies led to the arrest of thousands. It is believed on good evidence that his regime used torture and execution as dual means of eliminating any opposition for the most vocal while prison sentences were handed down to large numbers of less potent dissidents. Many people taken into custody simply disappeared and to this day there are no answers as to what happened to them.

Pinochet's rule was relentless. He tolerated no opposition. In 1976, the opposition leader, Orlando Letelier was blown up by a car bomb while he was in Washington, and the responsibility was laid at the doorstep of Pinochet's secret police. By 1978, Pinochet reconsidered his position and appointed a few civilian members to the cabinet, but this was only a token measure. In 1980, a new constitution was put out for public referendum, which guaranteed the existing regime power until 1989. It is believed that the vote results were never reported accurately since the constitution passed and Pinochet now had another eight-year term guaranteed.

Despite the police state actions, the Pinochet government did bring down inflation and did encourage investment and industrial growth because stability was assured through military rule. Foreign investors often see such tightly run dictatorships as profitable, a fact that flies in the face of human rights. But by 1982, the world entered a period of widespread recession and as a result, copper prices began to slump. As the Pinochet economic recovery began to be undermined by world events, tension between the people and the government rose. Tension grew to the point that Pinochet imposed a second state of emergency in late 1984; similar to the one he first imposed when coming to power. By September 1986, the government imposed drastic new repressions, as an unsuccessful attempt at assassination of the president showed that he was vulnerable. It was clear that conditions needed to change and even Pinochet himself knew that his days had to be numbered.

General Pinochet surprised the world when in 1988 he cancelled the state of emergency and asked for a public referendum as to whether his term should expire in March 1989 or be extended to 1997, giving him another eight-year term. The public vote was a resounding no with over half of the voters opposing his future holding of office. And this vote is assumed to have been even higher, but ballot tampering had to still have been a factor. Pinochet extended his term until March 1990 to allow for open presidential and congressional elections to be held.

Although the Christian Democrats won the election and chose Patricio Aylwin as the new president, General Pinochet announced that he would remain as commander and chief of the nation's armed forces, a position that would be hard to remove him from as long as the military remained loyal to him. Presidente Aylwin did, however, begin investigations into human rights violations committed under the Pinochet regime, hopeful that the General would not again seize power. By 1993, the second free election was slated and Eduardo Frei Ruiz-Tagle became Chile's new president. He saw to the removal of the nine senators who held their seats by military appointment, enabling those seats to again be held by elected officials. During Frei's presidency, the former head of the Pinochet secret police and his deputy received prison sentences for their role in the 1976 assassination of Letelier in Washington. Although Pinochet protested, the Supreme Court upheld the convictions and the military backed down from taking any action against civilian rule.

The Frei government passed legislation that enabled citizens to reopen investigation in the 542 cases of those who had disappeared under military repression, but only if their families could present new evidence. This was a bold step because once again the military could have thwarted the civilian efforts, but it did not.

In January 2001, Augusto Pinochet, then 85 years of age and in frail health, was charged with responsibility for at least 75 known political murders in which the victims were put to death in the most cruel of manners. This charge came as based upon testimony of General Joaquin Lagos after Pinochet himself denied having ever given any such orders. This revelation shocked the nation, and it came after Pinochet, who had gone to England for medical treatment, was arrested in London in 1998 based upon warrants from Spain that accused him of having ordered the murder of Spanish civilians in Chile. But rather than extradite him to Spain for trial, the British courts sent him back to Chile where he was placed under house arrest pending further investigation. All the while, General Pinochet continued to claim his innocence. At first Pinochet refused to cooperate with the court, but the then current commander of the military, General Ricardo Izurieta insisted that he comply with all court orders or he would loose any sympathy and support he still had among the military. This was an amazing turnaround from the initial reaction in Chile when he was arrested in London in 1998. At that time thousands of Chilenos still surprisingly supported the belief in his innocence.

The courts ordered that Pinochet undergo medical evaluation to see if he was competent to stand trial. The findings revealed that he was suffering from mild dementia as well as several physical ailments, but he was not in such diminished capacity as to be exempt from trial.

The cases against Augusto Pinochet and other military officers continued for the next several years. Although many officers were been imprisoned for their actions, General Pinochet, who by now was 90 years old, remained under house arrest while appeals kept being filed on his behalf. In 2006, at age 91, Pinochet died, but the people of Chile saw some measure of justice, and the nation recovered from this darkest of chapters in its tortured history. As for the fate of the missing, most of the cases remain unresolved. No doubt many of the perpetrators have gone unpunished, but they too are reaching old age. What would be gained by knowledge of the grizzly details of torture and murder, and what good would it do to punish officers who are nearing the end of their lives. So the people of Chile press on with the business of developing their nation and working to strengthen their democracy that has been so hard won.

On January 15, 2006, Dr. Michelle Bachelet was elected President of Chile. She became the first woman to win the presidency, and she promised a new day for the role of women in Chile. She was a Socialist and a survivor of the brutality of the Pinochet regime, having treated patients who were tortured under his regime. Sebastián Piñera succeeded her in 2010, well remembered for his care and devotion shown to the trapped miners who were so daringly rescued from deep underground. After his tenure, Michelle Bachelet ran again in 2014 and was reelected for another four-year term with a strong majority of the vote.

The Chileno constitution has undergone many changes since it was first initiated shortly after independence. The new constitution of 1980 has been amended in 1989, 1993 and 1997. Given the country's past instabilities, it is hard to say if the present constitution will be the same one governing the country far into the future. Essentially Chile is a republic with an executive branch of government, a bicameral legislature and a separate judiciary that is supposed to be free of political influence.

The current political process in Chile is one of mixed interests, very much unlike that of the United States where only two political parties hold power. In present day Chile, the Christian Democrat Party, the National Renewal Party, the Party for Democracy, the Socialist Party, the Independent Democratic Union and the Radical Social Democratic Party are all capable of electing members to the Congreso, and equally capable of placing a president in power. This means that a majority government is often hard to be achieved. The Communist Party, presently quite small, has not won a congressional seat in the past four elections. All citizens over the age of 18 are allowed to vote regardless of gender. Foreign persons who are legal residents may vote after living in Chile for five years without first becoming citizens.

The President of Chile is elected at large by popular vote for a term of six years, however, as noted above the multiplicity of political parties almost negates a candidate receiving 50 percent or more of the vote unless the individual is immensely popular. The president is both the head of state and the chief executive officer of the cabinet. The president then appoints his/her cabinet, each member carrying a portfolio of an important government ministry, or what Americans call a department. Combined they constitute the executive branch of government. In the past, the military often would seize power and suspend the role of the legislature, ruling by executive decree.

The Congreso is divided into two houses, the upper house known as the Senate and the lower house known as the Chamber of Deputies. The 48 senators are elected regionally and serve a term of 8 years, but their terms are staggered so that they are not all elected at the same time, half being elected every four years. There are nine seats that are designated members rather than elected. Two of the senate seats are held for former presidents, as once their term is finished they are entitled to a seat in the senate for life, providing they have served for at least six years as president. The Chamber of Deputies contains 120 seats, with members elected for terms of only four years.

The congressional election system in Chile is known as binomial. In each electoral district for the Senate and the Chamber of Deputies there are two seats up for election. If a coalition wins the majority of votes in that district, they share the seats. If, however, one of the coalition members wins the election by a two to one majority within the slate of candidates, then that party takes both seats.

Although Santiago is the national capital city of Chile, the Congreso meets in Valparaiso, the country's third largest city, which is located on the South Pacific Coast about 75 miles west of Santiago. The executive branch of government has its offices in the old national palace known as La Moneda, located in the heart of downtown Santiago. It is an imposing palatial building, but one unfortunately that has seen its share of military takeovers. All major government departments are located in Santiago, and it is where all foreign embassies are to be found.

The legal code for Chile is based upon the Code of 1857 essentially a derivative of Spanish law, but heavily influenced by the French Napoleonic code and Austrian law. At present Chile is in the process of changing its criminal justice system toward that of the American adversarial system whereby the defendant can challenge the state's evidence against him/her.

The Supreme Court of Chile, known as the Corte Suprema, is the highest authority on the law and decisions handed down by the Congreso. The judges are appointed by the president and ratified by the Senate just as is done in the United States. However, the list of candidates is provided to the president by the court itself, rather than the candidates being political appointees. The president of the court, similar to the American chief justice, is elected from within the 21-member court itself.

Below the Supreme Court, the Chileno judicial system has a court of appeals as well as a separate military judicial system. During the prosecution of those under the Pinochet regime who committed atrocities, there was some conflict of interest between the civilian and military courts as to jurisdiction, as those being indicted were military officers.

For general judicial purposes, Chile is divided into 13 districts. The courts of these districts are overseen by "intendentes" who are appointed to their positions. For general governmental administration, the districts are divided into provinces, each administered by an appointed governor, but municipalities within each province are governed over by elected mayors. Provinces in Chile do not have either the autonomy or the significance, as do American states or Argentine provinces. They would be more akin to counties in American states with regard to their overall function.

The Chileno military consists of the Army of the Nation, National Navy (which possesses its own air wing, operates the Coast Guard and Marine Corps), the Chileno Air Force and the Chileno Carabineros or national police force. All Chileno men between the ages of 18 and 45 are eligible for military conscription, a service of two years for army and four years for the navy or air force. Although Chile is somewhat isolated from the rest of South America by the Andes Mountains, the government spends over $3.4 billion dollars annually to maintain its military forces, a rather sizeable sum for a nation with just over 17,000,000 people.

Now that the atrocities of the Pinochet regime are behind them, the Chileno people hope to continue to administer their affairs in a democratic manner, operating under the principles of law and justice.

In 2019, Chile will hold presidential elections. The current president, Michelle Bachelet, will not be able to run again since consecutive terms are not permitted. She has been a powerful influence after having served in two separate four-year terms.

A statue of General Bernardo O'Higgins, liberator of Chile and the country's first president from 1818 to 1823

A formal portrait of Presidente Jorge Montt.

2015 earthquake damage (Work of Jorge Barrios CC-BY-SA 30 Wikimedia Commons)

Miners trapped deep underground for 69 days, (Hugo Infante/Government of Chile)

Dr. Michelle Bachelet, current President of Chile to 2018 (Compliments of the Ministerío Secretaria General de Gobierno de Chile)

CHILENO LIFESTYLE

A country like Chile that spans such diverse environmental zones and one that possesses numerous European cultures is bound to have developed both national as well as regional characteristics that make it distinct from its neighbors. Is there a Chileno way of life? Are there specific Chileno values? The answer in both cases is a resounding yes. Just as was seen in Argentina, Chile is a unique country with its own personality. This chapter looks into the various aspects of life in Chile to help you better appreciate the people and their culture, as you travel through the country.

CHILENO CITIES: Chile is an urban nation, but not a country dominated over by numerous big cities. Like most South American nations, Chile has one major city, but unlike other large countries, it does not have any other truly big cities. The remaining urban centers are for the most part quite small, having populations of around 100,000 people or less with only three exceptions.

Santiago is both the national capital and largest city in Chile. Its population of 7,200,000 accounts for approximately 30 percent of the national population. Concepción with 949,000 and Valparaiso with 930,000 people are the only other major cities in Chile. Valparaiso is the country's primary seaport and it serves the central valley region dominated over by Santiago. Essentially the two are linked to the degree that without Santiago, Valparaiso would not have much significance. Other regional centers are small, none coming anywhere near Concepción or Valparaiso in size.

Chile is a modern country, one whose social infrastructure is heavily dominated by people from northern and central Europe as well as the Iberian Peninsula. This duality of personalities is seen in the urban landscape of Chile.

In the south, wood tends to be the primary building material for housing, and in smaller towns it is also used for commercial buildings. But this is a rather recent trend, as Chilenos once considered wood to be the material of choice for poor people. Earlier fine quality homes even in the south were made of cement blocks and mortar, not the best material for earthquake country, but when well built they do stand up to strong tremors. There is a distinctly Germanic or Scandinavian look about the communities rather than one that speaks to Iberia. The style of housing reflects the tastes of the Germanic cultures rather than the Romanic, giving southern Chileno towns a look that is not in any way Latin American, most noticeable by the steeply pitched roofs, which are also in part an answer to the rains.

In the north, which is the Atacama Desert region, there is a stucco or concrete block houses with pitched roofs and those with flat roofs that are more akin to the American Southwestern style, thus reflecting a Spanish influence. But even in the desert north, the flavor of Chileno cities and towns is decidedly more European than what one would find across the border in Peru or Bolivia. Yes the church facing the plaza is found in northern towns, and yes the style reflects a trace of the Spanish Baroque, but the remainder of these towns is a mix of Germanic and Hispanic.

In the central portion of the country there is more of the Spanish influence because of the mild Mediterranean climate, which encouraged the initial settlement from Spain. But even here, the mix of various European cultures can be seen in the architectural patterns found. The most dominant city of the central valley region is Santiago, and its distinctive character will be discussed later in greater detail. Santiago is a major city of over 7,200,000 people. It is very modern, laid out with an essential grid pattern and is dominated over by middle-income housing. This is, however, true throughout Chile. Poverty does exist, but unlike most of Latin America, the massive barrios filled with peasant people who have come to the city and who are living in squalor is not seen in Chile, but there are a few small barrios that are decidedly poor and unkempt. Like Argentina, this is a country with a decidedly middle class population, rich and poor being equally in the minority.

Rural poverty in Chile is equally minimal, most farmers being rather prosperous and their farm homes contain many basic amenities that we would consider necessary to everyday life. Many of the larger estancias have magnificent homes, these dating to the days of the great landowners.

In the major cities, especially in Santiago, high-rise living is quite well accepted, despite the high earthquake frequency in the country. Massive blocks of apartments or condominiums abound throughout Santiago, are found in Valparaiso and in particular in Viña del Mar, Chile's great beach resort. Even in smaller cities and towns there are the occasional high-rise apartment or condominium block. Housing is quite affordable by North American standards with a nice house selling for under $100,000.

In all Chileno cities, the downtown area, known as centro, is still the center of the city. The downtown is always the focal point for government, higher education, the church and most of all for commercial purposes. The people of Chile have not developed the massive suburban sprawl as seen in the United States, thus downtown is still the hub for shopping, dining, entertainment and sport.

The central downtown of Chileno cities abounds with small shops, large stores similar to our department stores and a myriad of eateries that range from elegant restaurants to local lunch counters. There are always crowds of shoppers and office workers on breaks that throng the streets. In Santiago some of the downtown streets are strictly reserved for pedestrian traffic only. The shopping mall has not yet come to dominate in Chile; however, in Santiago, Valparaiso and the other major cities they do exist along with the supermarket.

HOME LIFE AND FAMILY: Chilenos are a very family oriented traditional people. The strong European and Iberian roots run deep, and family values are still important to these people. In rural areas, there are still many old traditions that date back to colonial times, especially on the estancias where ranch traditions involving horsemanship still prevail. Yet despite old traditional values, Chile is a very modern country with one of the highest literacy rates in the entire world. Its population is essentially young, with over three quarters of the people being under the age of 40. Although Spanish traditions do essentially prevail, the mixed European immigrant population since World War II has added many Germanic, Italian and British Isles influences. Although predominantly Roman Catholic, various Protestant faiths are also intermingled. However, unlike Argentina, there is a greater degree of homogeneity in Chile, as European immigration outside of Iberia has not been as totally dominant. Chileno society is essentially free from ethnic strife, the greatest distinction being made between the more urban sophisticates and those from rural areas. Poverty does exist, but it is in no way grinding or as debilitating as in other Latin American countries. Chile is not a nation in which the illiterate poor of the country flock to the cities to improve their lot.

Among intellectual Chilenos there has always been a strong interest in the French flavor of life. There is a level of urban sophistication found in Santiago, Valparaiso and Viña del Mar that is akin to what can be seen in Buenos Aires. Although Santiago is not considered to be a second Paris as is true of Buenos Aires, the upper and middle class people do mirror many of the daily traits of French society. Family gatherings are very gracious affairs, accompanied by elegant cuisine and wine, served on fine china and in an atmosphere that reflects values not seen in those countries where the lifestyle has a more indigenous influence. In southern Chile, the family values and close ties of the Germanic community are built upon parental respect and close sibling interaction. It is not uncommon to see large family gatherings outdoors during the summer months, again with lavish amounts of food being served.

Although American influences can be seen in such things as fashion, the introduction of fast food, cinema and music, these influences have not had an immediate impact upon family life. Chilenos still place great value upon family ties. Children still spend time with parents, and the home is still the focus of social life. One distinct element of life in the Chileno home is a love of the night. Chilenos are a nocturnal people. It is not uncommon for family gatherings or dinner parties to last well into the early morning hours. Of course, the main meal is generally not served until around eight or nine in the evening.

FOOD AND MUSIC: The cuisine of Chile is a fusion of Spanish and other European cultures with little or no indigenous influences. Unlike many other Latin American countries, hot and spicy is not totally dominant in Chile. The common form of flavoring is the use of garlic and onion, but this is not to say that the proverbial chili is absent. It is used, but not to the degree that we normally associate with Latin American food.

In Chile there is a strong use of meat, but nothing as dominant as the Argentine asado. Roasted meats are popular, often the meat being flavored with the use of carrots and onion imbedded into the meat so that when it is cut, the colors and taste of the vegetables are part of each slice. The empanada is the most popular luncheon dish. This pastry turnover is filled with various meats, potatoes or vegetables and often topped with a garnish of avocado. Empanadas are available everywhere, and they are to Chile what the hamburger is to America. But Chilenos do have one fast food item that is a heart attack waiting to happen. The completo is a long hot dog served on a large bun, topped with mayonnaise, mashed avocado, chopped tomato, sauerkraut, green chili and shredded cheese. I would simply label it a "cholesterol pig out." But they are popular.

Seafood is also a popular item in Chile given that the country has such an extensive coastline. Sea bass is one of the most sought after dishes, often seared with fresh garlic and served with a rich sauce made from black beans, or a buttery sauce with almonds and pistachios. Fish soups and stews are also very popular in Chile. One dish that is quite popular is a stew of fish, shellfish, chicken pork, lamb, beef and potatoes. It is somewhat similar to the Portuguese or Spanish paella, but with a Chileno twist.

The most popular comfort food in Chile is *pastel de chocolo*. This is a casserole made with chicken or meat, combined with olives, raisins and hard boiled eggs then topped with a mixture of corn meal, sugar and butter. The casserole is baked and then brought to the table piping hot.

On cold winter nights the people of Chile often warm up with a soup made from the cranberry bean, potatoes, corn and squash. Vegetable dishes are important accompaniment to any meal, including marinated tomatoes and other vegetables.

For dessert, the Chileno list is very long. The central and eastern European influences are very strong. Some of the most delicious chocolate tortes you will find anywhere are to be found in Chile. Many pastries involve the use of fresh or cooked fruits, and the Chileno bakers are masters at tempting one's palate with varied flavors.

Chile is a country filled with folk music. There are many popular singers and dance troupes that keep alive the traditions of the past, even touring foreign countries. There is a lilting quality to the music, string instruments accompanying the vocal or dance, showing the strength of the Spanish influence. Songs vary in their subject matter, but not surprisingly the sea is a popular theme. The guitar is also the most common background instrument in Chileno music, giving it a soft and subtle quality. The rhythm is subtle unlike the strong tango beat that is found in Argentine music. Dancers wear costumes that often reflect the influences of the great estancias, and again are reminiscent of those found in Spain. In one popular dance called the Cueca, both the men and women accompany their movements with the waving of long scarves, adding to the seductive quality of the dance itself.

There are many festivals that take place across Chile, some being religious in nature while others celebrate the harvest, the changing seasons or pay tribute to the folk culture and music of the country.

URBAN SOPHISTICATION VS. RURAL SIMPLICITY: The people of Santiago, Valparaiso and Viña del Mar do lead lives that are more detached from the land, based upon more European values. Urban sophistication is comparable to that of Europe, but yet the people who live this lifestyle are not that far removed from the country's rural roots. In Santiago, the snow covered Andes look down upon the city, and their lower foothills are less than a half-hour drive from the heart of the city. The central valley region in which Santiago is located is the heart of the country's diverse Mediterranean agriculture, thus people in the city can take a drive into the country, visit a winery, attend a local fiesta or shop for fresh produce from roadside stands in a matter of minutes. Along the coast, those who live in the Valparaiso area have much open country with beautiful beaches that are beyond the urban horizon, or they can cross the low coastal hills and also enjoy the landscapes and availability of activities in the central valleys.

Away from the heartland of the country, the smaller cities and towns of Chile are close to the land, thus although people may lead urban lives, they are more closely attached to the rural traditions and festivals that grew with the country from its earliest colonial beginnings.

CHILENO TRANSPORTATION SERVICES: Chile possesses a good highway network of sealed roads that extend from its northern border with Peru and Bolivia all the way south to Puerto Montt. At this far southern location the coastline bends eastward, approaching the Andes. The various fast flowing rivers, deep inlets and fjords make road building virtually impossible, especially given the small and scattered population. Thus southern Chile is virtually devoid of a highway network, however, there are some sealed roads that connect coastal communities with their counterparts across the mountains in far southern Argentina, and then re cross the border back into Chile to connect Punta Arenas and Puerto Natal with the rest of the country via a major detour through the Argentine region of Patagonia.

In the central valley region, the road network is excellent. There are major four-lane divided freeways, including one interstate type highway that connects Santiago with Valdivia located to the south. There is also one major route that crosses the high Andes, connecting Santiago with Mendoza and all points east in Argentina. This major highway crosses the border at an altitude of over 10,000 feet, making this one of the highest major international ports of entry in the Western Hemisphere.

It is easy to travel to most parts of Chile where roads exist utilizing the bus. Long distance busses are very modern, clean and efficient and connect most parts of the country with the capital. One will not find the typical broken down bus with chickens and livestock as would be seen in some Andean countries.

Chile also possesses a network of railway lines that connect all of the major cities of the country with Santiago, but as in so many countries, the railway network handles freight today rather than passengers. At one time, Chile maintained a more extensive passenger rail service, but like so many countries that have modernized, the private automobile has made rail travel less popular. Once it was even possible to cross the Andes by train, connecting Buenos Aires with Santiago, but today that journey can be made by air in less than three hours. There is still one passenger train per day operating between Santiago and Concepción and Temuco, a distance of around 400 miles. Metrotren is a commuter service that operates in the greater Santiago region, offering efficient and comfortable service to communities that are as far from the capital as 100 miles. Metrotren maintains a number of routes and provides quite regular service to connect the hinterlands with the capital. And the city of Santiago possesses a fast and efficient subway system for travel within the city, the most extensive system in South America. There is also a fleet of city busses to provide additional service, and this holds true in all of the larger cities of Chile.

LAN Chile Airlines is the nation's primary air carrier, connecting Chile with other countries within South America. In addition LAN Chile offers service from Santiago to the United States, Europe and Australia. It is a small airline by world standards, but it maintains a high level of service and safety. Chile's second national airline is Ladeco, competing with LAN Chile primarily for domestic and South American service routes. Air travel within Chile is practical given the vast distances between Santiago and cities to either the north or south. Travel south of Puerto Montt is almost always accomplished by air.

CHILENO SPORTS: Chile is a country of such diverse environmental and cultural characteristics, so naturally there should be a great variation in the types of sporting activities available. With a rib of mountains running the entire length of the country, trekking into the foothills and lower slopes is a popular pastime. Chilenos have a passion for their mountains and especially for the central and southern forests.

Trekking and camping are very popular weekend and vacation activities.

One of the most beloved of pastimes dates back to the 18th century when Catholic monks introduced kites to the country. During spring and summer, when breezes are just right, kite flying is a pastime that is enjoyed by young and old alike. In parks across the country, people are out to savor this simple but favored sport.

Another distinctly Chileno game is rayuela. Men play it most often, but the range in ages can be from childhood to old age. A metal disk, known as a tejo, somewhat like a discus, is thrown down a course. A string across the path of the tejo is the object of the game, as contestants aim to have their disk land right on the string.

A popular game that has its origin among Chile's indigenous population is known as chueca. There are some parallels to hockey, but in chueca the contestants first start in the middle of the field, attempting to knock a rubber ball into a hole using a curved stick. After one team succeeds, they then must drive the same ball down across a goal line at one end of the field in order to score while the opposing team tries to block their way.

The number one spectator sport in Chile, and also the number one sport played by school age children is soccer, known better as fútbol. The sport draws large crowds in every city or town across the country where two teams can come together. In the large Santiago stadium, crowds of 80,000 can be accommodated, and there is no difficulty in filling seats. And of course the world cup draws great attention in the country, especially when Chile is a contending nation.

In the rural areas, rodeo competition is still highly popular. Known as "la fiesta huasa," the Chileno cowboy or "huaso," is a figure to be admired by young children. Their dress is quite commanding, their bright ponchos, leggings, cowboy-type boots and spurs being capped by a flat-topped hat. Children admire them and women swoon over their handsome visage, but it is the actual competition itself that brings the crowd to its feet in cheers. Two man teams attempt to control the movements of a steer using their horses rather than getting down in the mud, as do American rodeo cowboys.

The horse is generally considered to be a part of the history and lore of Chile. Many thousands still enjoy the sport of horseback riding or even going on pack trips into the mountains. Likewise, polo is especially popular among the rich of the country. It is understandable given the nation's history that the horse plays an important role in rural Chileno life.

Among urbanites, golf and tennis are very popular sports, especially for the upper middle-income white-collar workers. And like in so many countries, jogging is popular among those who are health conscious.

With a major coastline, Chileno people enjoy their beaches and offshore waters as well as their inland glacial lakes. Boating, water skiing and fishing are all important activities. Deep-sea fishing and scuba diving or snorkeling are also very popular sports.

In general, Chilenos are more athletic than North Americans, enjoying their coastline and mountains alike. There seems to be no end to the varied sports available. Almost everyone engages in some type of outdoor activity, a lesson that others could certainly learn.

WINTER SPORTS: Chile is now a country in which winter sports have become popular. There are a few ski resorts located in the mountains east of Santiago and in the southern lake country, taking advantage of excellent conditions for the accumulation of heavy amounts of snow. Many European athletes come here during the Southern Hemisphere winter to gain an edge by practicing their winter skills while the Northern Hemisphere basks in summer. Although both Chile and Argentina have excellent ski resorts, their chances of ever hosting the winter Olympic games are slim because of the awkard time of year for winter athletes who are residents of the Northern Hemisphere.

The crowded skyline of Providencia in Santiago

Emerging from the Metro at the Bacquedando Station in downtown
Santiago

Historic European style post office in downtown Santiago

Changing the guard at the Casa Moneda, Chile's Presidential Palace

Popular beachfront in Viña del Mar on the Pacific

Wood housing is more typical in cold and windy Punta Arenas

There is a strong German cultural influence in the Lake District

High quality wine produced in the Colchaga Valley of Central Chile

Pastel de Chocolo, the national dish of Chile (Work of Diegostraight, CC BY SA 4.0, Wikimedia.org)

Passenger train arriving in San Fernando on its way north to Santiago

The hot spring resort of Jahuel north of Santiago

Portillo, on the Argentine border, is one of Chile's main ski resorts

LAND AND PEOPLE OF URUGUAY

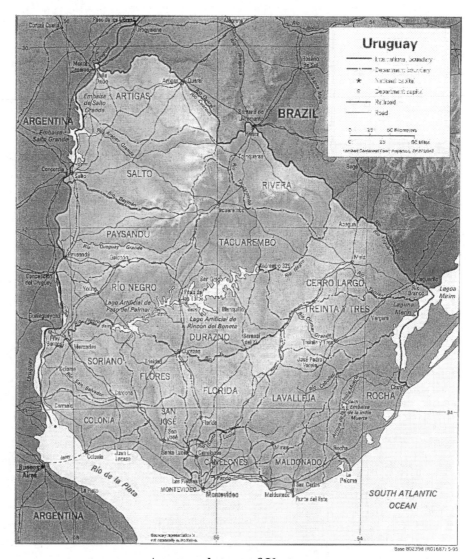

A general map of Uruguay

The vast majority of cruises around the Cone of South America that either leave Buenos Aires or follow an eastbound route from Valparaiso, Chile will include one to two port calls in Uruguay. Montevideo, the national capital and largest city and Punta del Este (Maldonado) are the two ports that major cruise lines will visit. Montevideo is an old city with a rich history, and its architectural flavor is somewhat like that of Buenos Aires, but with a decidedly more Latin American flavor. Punta del Este is a sparkling resort built on a narrow point of land that is an extension of the much older colonial city of Maldonado. Beach enthusiasts from Buenos Aires and from the cities of southern Brazil frequent Punta del Este. The Argentinos favor it because surprisingly there are few sandy beaches south of Buenos Aires. And the wealthy Brazilians enjoy Punta del Este because it is so free of crime, something that plagues urban beaches in Brazil.

Uruguay is one of the smallest countries on the continent, occupying a total land area of 176,215 square kilometers or 68,037 square miles and having a population of only 3,341,000 people. The land area is just slightly larger than England and Wales combined. Most of Uruguay is a continuation of the Pampas that extend across the Rio de la Plata from Argentina. This gives the country relatively flat, exceptionally fertile land. The original natural cover was tall grass dotted with groves of broadleaf trees. Only in the far north of the country does the land rise into moderate hills, the highest elevations only reaching 1,688 feet above sea level. And here there is a slight increase in the ground cover, essentially woodland. The climate is humid sub tropical with warm summers and cool winters. Rainfall is generous and severe storms are rare. Snowfall in the interior is equally rare, occurring once every few decades.

Several major rivers that rise in the southern Brazilian Highlands cross Uruguay on their way to the Rio de la Plata or the Rio Paraná, providing for hydroelectric potential as well as irrigation to augment the natural rainfall when necessary.

This is a highly prosperous land, agriculture being the mainstay of the economy. Uruguay produces wheat and other grains, raises beef and dairy cattle and has a thriving wine producing industry as well as being noted for its wide variety of fruits and vegetables. With a small population, food exports are very important to the Uruguayan economy. Essentially this is a country with limited manufacturing, relying heavily upon its fertility to provide for exports.

A VERY BRIEF HISTORY: The Portuguese did some exploration of the territory in 1512, followed by the Spanish in 1516. But neither saw any potential for mineral riches. But the Spanish did see the land as having a potential for raising cattle. It was the Spanish who first established a settlement in 1624. Portuguese later settled in Uruguay in 1680, establishing their colony along the Rio de la Plata at Colonia de Sacramento. Over the next century and a half, the two nations contested the land, each building forts and establishing settlements. By the early 1700's, the Spanish had developed the port of Montevideo, but later saw that it had a potential to compete with Buenos Aires.

During the Napoleonic War, the British were attempting to control the Rio de la Plata and actually occupied Montevideo in 1807, but their occupation was brief. By 1811, Spain was back in control and then faced a popular uprising in Uruguay that led to several battles culminating in 1815 with the rebel forces seizing Montevideo. But one year later Portuguese forces occupied the city in 1817. In essence Uruguay even in revolution became a pawn between Argentina and Brazil. Portugal lost Brazil in 1822, and the new Brazilian monarchy maintained its hold over the eastern provinces of Uruguay until 1828 when the British helped the Uruguayan people gain their independence from both Brazil and Argentina.

The 19th century saw struggle between opposing political forces, often including violence with intervention by Brazil, Britain and France in attempts to restore order. Between 1875 and 1886, the military took control and in essence created a modern nation out of Uruguay, encouraging economic development and immigration. And it was in this period that waves of various Europeans came to the country from Italy, Germany, Spain and France, creating a multi ethnic melting pot of Europeans similar to what happened in Argentina. The native population and those of mestizo origin (half native and half Spanish) became totally overshadowed by the European population and today Europeans make up over 88 percent of the population. Of the remaining 12 percent, a small number of people of African ancestry, descendants of former Brazilian slaves, do live in Uruguay.

In the early 20th century with civilian government restored, the country again reverted to violent confrontations between opposing political forces until the outset of World War II when the country stabilized. Although neutral during the war, the most famous incident was the granting sanctuary to the German pocket battleship Graf Spee, which had been damaged fighting the British. After the time limit for a neutral to allow a combatant in port, the captain of the Graf Spee took the ship back to sea and scuttled it rather than risk capture by the British. Many of its sailors and officers are buried in Montevideo and a prominent monument was erected in the port area and at the cemetery. This is in many ways a sad story, but also one of great courage and conviction on the part of the captain of the ship.

From 1968 to 1973, the country was in turmoil, with the military having established a joint civilian-military government from 1973 to 1985. Since 1985, the country has maintained democratic rule and its economy has also prospered, but primarily being one of food production and limited light manufacturing. Tourism has played an increasing role, especially in the beach areas along the eastern coast. As noted, Argentina does not have excellent beaches, so many Argentinos spend vacations in Uruguay, and there has also been a strong real estate boom with Brazilians and Argentinos buying homes or condominiums in the beach resorts, especially in Punta del Este. Brazil has outstanding beaches, but wealthy Brazilians feel more comfortable in Uruguay because crime is minimal, especially in resort areas, which stands in stark contrast to Brazil.

THE PEOPLE AND LIFESTYLE: I have a close personal friend who is Uruguayan, and I have visited the country on many occasions. I have been fortunate enough to spend a lot of time with my friend and her family and associates, therefore I feel very comfortable speaking to a country's culture and lifestyle. Uruguayans are culturally much closer to Argentinos than to Brazilians. They do, however, in great numbers speak Portuguese as a second language because of their proximity to Brazil and the great number of Brazilians who visit the country's beach resorts. When it comes to speaking Spanish, the dialect and accent of the Uruguayan Spanish is almost identical to that of the Argentine Spanish.

There is only one major city in Uruguay, and that is Montevideo. It bears a lot of similarity in its small city core to Buenos Aires, yet in its residential areas it lacks the large numbers of apartment towers that are seen in the Argentine counterpart. Only along the beachfront are there concentrations of high-rises, but they are nowhere as tall or widespread. Most of Montevideo is a city of single-family houses, the older style having flat roofs, few windows facing the street and interior courtyards being the focus of the house. Newer suburban homes have a very North American flavor, most constructed of red brick and being more spacious in the ranch style. Because of lower crime rates, no major walls or barriers are seen facing the streets and there is a more open feel to the neighborhoods. The eastern end of the city is the more upscale part of Montevideo with the less expansive west side being older and more lower to middle income oriented. There are only a few small true barrios on the north and far west sides of the city, reflecting the country's more middle class average population. As a smaller city,

Montevideo has only public bus service, as there has never been any need to build an underground Metro.

Family plays as much a role in the daily lives of the people of Uruguay as is true in Argentina and Chile. With their strong European background, the home is very much the center of family and social life. When you are invited to someone's home in Uruguay, you can count on being entertained in a gracious manner, and that often revolves around a lavish meal. Families prepare copious amounts of food when they gather, especially when guests are invited. There will be a beautiful table prepared with a variety of appetizers and salads, followed by the main course that is usually grilled meats or fresh seafood. And then dessert follows later in the evening.

There is great respect shown within the Uruguayo family for age and position. This is an outgrowth of Old World traditions that place great emphasis upon the prestige brought to a family by those who attain positions in the community of respect such as teachers, lawyers, doctors or government leaders. And age is always greatly respected with family elders held in high esteem.

Among rural families, there is a great love of and respect for the land. Old families that have held estancias for generations are still considered to be local patrons and are generally looked up to. Today many estancias have diversified into agricultural pursuits, especially the production of fine wines.

CULTURAL LIFE: The people of Uruguay have a great love of life. Dining out, going to the beach, taking outings into the countryside and traveling are all very important, especially if personal incomes permit. There is also a great love of music and the arts. Folk music, classical concert music, ballet and theater are all important, especially among the urban dwellers of Montevideo. And like Argentina, Tango plays a very important role in the culture of Uruguay.

GOVERNMENT: Uruguay is a democratic nation that shows great political stability today, though in the past it has seen its share of turmoil. The country elects both a president and members for the General Assembly or parliament. All terms are for five-years and all adult citizens are encouraged to vote. There are no separate provincial or state administrations and all services are provided by the national government.

The General Assembly is divided into two chambers. The Chamber of Deputies made up of 99 members represents the country's 19 departments, which are not in effect provinces. The seats are allocated based upon population. The Senate consists of 31 members who also represent proportional distribution.

The judicial system is also national with the Corta Suprema being selected by the General Assembly. They in turn select the judges of the lower courts.

One unique aspect of the governmental structure of Uruguay is that any changes to the national constitution or in repealing any undesired laws is left to the people by means of national referendum.

SPORTS: Uruguay is a nation in which futbol, or what we call soccer, is king. It is considered to be the national sport and is enjoyed with great relish. When local teams or the national team play, the games are a major event. There is also a great love for the various types of competitions held out on the estancias, what in North America would amount to rodeo. And being a country where the majority of people live along the coast, water sports and sailing are very popular with locals as well as visitors.

The rural landscape north of Montevideo where vineyards are developing

The very popular beachfront of Punta del Este

A monument to the early history of pioneer life in Uruguay

Visitors enjoy the architecture and flavor of Old Montevideo

The celebration of national Police Day to honor those who serve

Elegant high-rise apartments along Positos Beach in Montevideo

BUENOS AIRES

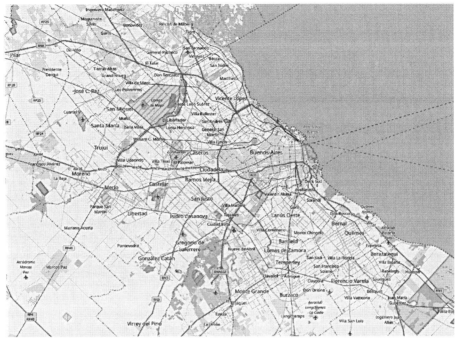

**The greater region of Buenos Aires located along the Rio de La Plata
(© OpenStreetMap contributors)**

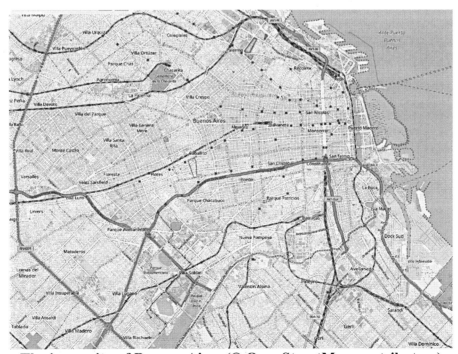

The inner city of Buenos Aires (© OpenStreetMap contributors)

Buenos Aires, the capital and largest city of Argentina, is one of the truly great world cities both in size and its level of culture and sophistication. This is without question the premier city of South America, despite being second in size to São Paulo, Brazil. Buenos Aires with all of its suburbs has a metropolitan population of over 15,200,000, making it as large as Los Angeles, but fortunately it is more compact in physical size.

HOW LONG AND WHERE TO STAY: I strongly recommend several days in Buenos Aires either before or after the cruise. To miss this incredible and vibrant city is to loose out on a wonderful cultural experience. Travel writers and visitors alike do not call Buenos Aires "The Paris of the Americas" without good cause. There is more of a European flavor than there is that of Latin America, yet despite being heavily European, Buenos Aires is its own distinct entity. The city has a flavor and "vibe" that makes it so distinctive, and so different from the more staid and conservative attitude of cities in the United States, Canada, Australia or the United Kingdom.

If you plan to stay a few nights in Buenos Aires, I strongly urge you to choose one of the five-star hotels because these offer luxury, convenience and security. I do not mean that crime is a major problem to worry about such as would be true in Rio de Janeiro, but as a metropolis, there is a degree petty crime such as pickpocketing and hotel burglary that you will not experience in one of the top hotels. The other factor to consider is the language barrier unless you are fluent in Spanish. At four and five-star hotels, English is widely spoken by the staff since a vast majority of guests are from North America and Western Europe. But as the number of stars drops on the rating, there is less likelihood of English being widely spoken.

There are many hotel choices in all price ranges, but for maximum convenience and the ability to absorb the true spirit that is Buenos Aires, I strongly urge you to stay in the suburban districts of Retiro or Recoleta, as here is where you will find the greatest restaurants, night life, street life and overall ambiance. Although it is considered suburban, it is only blocks from the very heart of the city where there are so many venues to be seen. The hotels that I highly recommend are:
* Alvear Palace - This five-star hotel is legendary for its Old World charm and gracious service. It is situated in the heart of Recoleta, the most fashionable district within the city where so many dining and shopping venues are located. At 1895 Alvear Avenue, you will be able

to walk to a wide variety of important venues and great restaurants. Plus the hotel itself is noted for fine dining.

*Four Seasons Buenos Aires - This high-rise hotel is both modern and traditional, providing impeccable five-star service, elegant dining and superb views from most of its guest rooms. Located at Posadas 1086/88, many rooms face north out to the grand boulevard 9 de Julio where you get commanding views of the city skyline.

* Park Hyatt Buenos Aires - Another superb five-star hotel in Recoleta is this great Hyatt property at 1661 Alvear Avenue. The hotel combines Old World charm with modern amenities and elegant service, providing impeccable dining and touring options. I would have to rate it as my first choice

Of the more moderate, but still well recognized hotels, I have three to offer in my recommendations:

* Alvear Art Hotel - This new Alvear property differs from the Alvear Palace in that it is very modern and provides more of a so called "hip" atmosphere that many younger up market guests find appealing. It is very well located at Suipacha 1036 just a block off of Avenida 9 de Julio and two blocks from Plaza San Martin.

* Hilton Buenos Aires - This is a four-star Hilton property, located in Puerto Madero at Avenida Muchada Guemes 351 is a very "glitzy" new hotel that is in the middle of one of the most rapidly developing waterfront districts of the city. But it is a fair walk to get into the heart of the city and too far to walk to the Recoleta or Retiro districts so favored by foreign visitors.

*Hotel Sofitel Buenos Aires - This four-star property is across the street from Retiro Station, the main suburban railway station serving the northern part of the city. It offers both an Old World atmosphere and new world amenities and is in very close proximity to both the downtown core and Recoleta.

* Sheraton Libertador - This excellent Sheraton property is located at Avenida Cordoba 690, which is in the bustling heart of the city. It has more of a business atmosphere because of its centrality where it is adjacent to many other high-rise building and in a high traffic locale.

THE ESSENCE OF BUENOS AIRES: Buenos Aires, which means "Good Air" in Spanish, is located on the wide estuary of the Paraná River, known as the Rio de la Plata, so often mistakenly called "The River Plate" by many English speakers. This broad salt-water estuary separates the coast of Argentina from that of Uruguay, and at Buenos Aires it is about 30 to 50 miles wide. The city is actually at the eastern end of the Pampas and is therefore situated on flat ground, primarily grassland, but dotted with trees and shrubs, especially around watercourses. Climatically it has a humid sub-tropical climate, similar in nature to that of the American city of Charleston, South Carolina. Summers are warm and humid, occasionally experiencing temperatures in the upper 20's to low 30's Celsius or 80's or low 90's Fahrenheit. Winters are cool, with storms sweeping across the Pampas bringing blustery conditions and plenty of rain. Snow in Buenos Aires is not a commonplace occurrence, happening decades apart. Hurricanes do not occur in the waters of the South Atlantic Ocean.

The central city is laid out with a basic grid pattern that follows an axis of the broad park lined boulevards Avenida 9 de Julio and Avenida de Mayo. There are angled streets that radiate out from the central city into the surrounding suburbs. Essentially the city grew adjacent to the waterfront, as from its earliest inception Buenos Aires has been a port city. The port plays so much of a role in the city's history, that Buenos Aires residents are known as Porteños, meaning people of the port.

In stark contrast to North American cities including those in the Canadian province of Québec, Buenos Aires reflects an architectural flavor that speaks to that of Paris. Not only does the city possess elegantly manicured parks, grand boulevards and public monuments, but the inner city is liberally laced with late 19th century apartment blocks that are patterned after those found in the French capital. Then from the 1930's on, Buenos Aires saw the construction of hundreds of high-rise apartment and condominium towers, most with the distinct art deco style, which was common to both New York and Chicago at that time. Since World War II, as the city has continued to grow, the architectural pattern for high-rise has been that of the contemporary glass and steel type construction. Thus there are three layers of dense high-rise buildings that comprise almost the entire central city. Essentially Buenos Aires has more high-rise buildings than New York City, a density and distribution that makes it one of the most densely settled cities in the world, but unlike New York City the buildings in Buenos Aires are not higher than 20 to 30 stories. This gives Buenos Aires a most dramatic skyline, as in the central business district and Puerto Madero there are many quite tall buildings. The city is upon first glance almost overwhelming, due to its tight clustering of high-density construction.

There is an overall vitality that one can feel when walking through the streets of Buenos Aires; similar to that one feels in Paris or Madrid. The sidewalks are broad and thronged with well-dressed people.

Sidewalk cafes abound, and everywhere there are parks or plazas filled with benches that enable people to enjoy the out of doors while being in the heart of a major urban center. The Plaza San Martin, grand Plaza de Mayo and the massive green belt that is the Avenida 9 de Julio, lend an atmosphere of elegance to the central downtown area.

The Avenida 9 de Julio is actually the world's widest boulevard. It is so broad that a pedestrian needs two to three changes of traffic lights to be able to cross the entire street. Two broad green belts, impeccably maintained, separate the major traffic lanes. In addition, there are two outermost lanes from the through inner lanes, about 16 in total. In the middle there are now special lanes for busses, two in each direction with the bus stops under covered stations in the middle. It intersects with the Avenida de Mayo, which has its eastern end at the Plaza de Mayo fronting on the Casa Rosada, or presidential palace and its western end at the Congreso, or national parliament. This is essentially the very heart of the city and everything of importance is found within a mile or two off of these two primary streets.

Unlike American cities, Buenos Aires does not have a concentrated downtown. The city center is a mix of residential and shopping districts that are integrated with parks, plazas and government buildings, and the area spreads over many square miles The Calle Florida is a pedestrian oriented shopping street, and if any single street could be called the heart of the city's commercial activities, this would be it. The Calle Florida is a narrow pedestrian only street, and it is lined with a myriad of small shops and major stores, providing one of the most concentrated retail districts of any world city. One can buy almost anything on this street, especially in the realm of high quality merchandise. Buenos Aires central district is known for its designer clothing, excellent leather coats, bags and shoes and fine European jewelry. Calle Florida is also home to many fine restaurants, but the entire central city is dotted with high quality eateries, many being small cafes or bistros, and many having exterior dining facilities. It is not uncommon to see a young couple dancing Tango with the music of a boom box, placing a hat or dish alongside to receive contributions. All along Calle Florida the music of Tango can be heard on almost every block.

Traffic in the inner city is quite heavy, and it is often said that if one can survive driving in central Buenos Aires traffic, one can drive anywhere. But that same saying applies to Rome, Paris and many other major world capital cities. I personally thought traffic was quite orderly and drivers appear to obey the traffic lights. But pedestrians be warned - do not try and cross outside of a designated intersection or crosswalk, as drivers will not stop for you. This can be frustrating, but take heed and do not ever try to cross in the middle of a block even though you may see some locals doing it.

Most first time visitors to Buenos Aires, especially North American tourists, are amazed at the fast pace, the crowded streets and sidewalks and the liveliness of the city. They are also somewhat mesmerized by the diversity of its architecture, both old and new crowded together in a 'cheek by jowl" fashion. For those who love architecture, the older buildings of Buenos Aires offer plenty of so called eye candy. The city center is so reminiscent of the late 19th and early 20th century styles in central Paris or Madrid.

LA BOCA AND SAN TELMO: The southern waterfront district of Buenos Aires is known as La Boca, meaning "the mouth." This is essentially a poor part of the city, yet despite being a less than desirable neighborhood, it is a popular venue for visitors. It is here amid very colorful buildings constructed of wood, stucco, brick and sheet iron that tango was born. But most tango shows that tourists patronize are in the adjacent neighborhood of San Telmo, a late 18th and early 19th century colonial district of substantial and elegant buildings, mostly somewhat faded today There are many small nightclubs devoted to the dance that is synonymous with Argentina. And visitors can come to La Boca or San Telmo in relative safety during the daytime, but at night it is wise to not walk the streets without a guide or escort. In San Telmo there is a weekend flea market that brings shoppers from all parts of the city. And it is not uncommon to see tango demonstrations along the sidewalk during the day just as you see on Calle Florida.

La Boca evokes a spirit and charm that is unique to Buenos Aires. The houses are painted in multiple colors, often in gaudy shades that seem to be at odds with one another. And many walls are covered in murals, or what one would call organized graffiti. Behind La Boca there are many square miles of poor class housing, but essentially these neighborhoods do not dominate Buenos Aires, nor are they as lacking in facilities and services as would be seen in other major cities of Latin America. This in itself shows that the overall standard of living in Argentina is well above that of other Latin American countries with the exception of Chile and Uruguay

RETIRO AND RECOLETA: The wealthiest inner city neighborhoods are Retiro and Recoleta. These neighborhoods begin at the northern end of Avenida 9 de Julio, with Retrio being a district of hotels, apartment blocks, foreign embassies and small shopping arcades. This is considered a very desirable area in which to live because of its proximity to the city center, especially for young white-collar professionals. The architectural flavor of Retiro is a mix of mid to late 19th century along with modern high-rises packed quite close together. Farther north at some designated street that I could not determine, Retiro becomes Recoleta, which is considered to be even more up market. Visually it is imperceptible as to the eye what gives it any sense of difference from Retiro. However, at the center of Recoleta is a large walled in cemetery of the same name. But this is no ordinary cemetery. It is truly a "city of the dead," because it contains individual and family crypts, some being quite elaborate. And they line a grid of pedestrian streets in city fashion. A committee of wealthy old-line families that have plots in the cemetery can nix the burial of anyone they deem undesirable. When Eva Peron died, even though her husband was the dictatorial president, she was denied burial. It was not until nearly two decades later that Eva Peron be interred in the family crypt. And today it is the most visited grave and one of the highlights for many tourists to the city.

PALERMO AND BELGRANO: North of Recoleta and extending along the Rio de la Plata are the suburbs of Palermo and Belgrano, both essentially upscale and beautiful residential areas. Palermo is a very elegant district of high-rise apartments mixed with large single family homes. Belgrano contains the beautiful Paseo de Las Americas, Parque Tres de Febrero, Plaza Holanda, the Hipodromo Argentina de Palermo and Lago de Regatas - all major recreational facilities covering vast acreage. It is also home to the Estadio Monumental Antonio Vespucio Liberti and the Ciudad Universidad de Buenos Aires. It is also a district containing beautiful mansions and tall, very modern high-rise apartments.

These two neighborhoods are among the more popular with professionals who wish to live close to the heart of the city, but in an area where the streets are quiet and filled with shade trees. Traversing these two districts is Avenida Cabildo, which is both a major travel artery and an important street for all of the local types of shops needed to support a major residential community. And of course there are many local restaurants catering to local clientele.

TIGRE: Palermo and Belgano are both connected to the central city by means of the SubT (Metro) and the main commuter rail line that extends north into the outer suburb of Tigre where it ends. Although at the far northern edge of the city, Tigre has become quite popular for its water recreational facilities, as it is located on the actual delta land of the Rio Paraná before it enters the Rio de la Plata. The town is actually situated on an island, as several small rivers distribute water from the Rio Paraná, as it is breaking down into numerous distributary streams. There are many traditional older homes, modern high-rise apartments and newer small homes catering to a variety of income levels. There are also numerous nice small hotels and motor launch tour operators, as Tigre has also become a weekend getaway from the pace of the city.

OTHER SUBURBS: Buenos Aires is divided into dozens of distinctive suburban communities, each with its own principal shopping street and local character. The suburbs vary in their degree of interest, but primarily only to those who have a strong penchant for studying the layout, architecture and local conditions of urban life. For the average visitor, these vast suburban neighborhoods will hold little or no meaning and therefore are not worthy of individual note. The farther northwest, west and south one goes out of the central city, the less interesting the suburbs become. And many are actually home to lower income families, but fortunately most are still respectable, having paved streets, sidewalks and other basic urban amenities. These neighborhoods are far from the vast urban barrios you would find in Lima, Bogota or Mexico City, though there are a handful of such enclaves Unless you speak fluent Spanish and specifically dresses down, hides their camera and is very cautious, it is unwise to travel into these parts of the city on your own.

GETTING AROUND THE CITY: You will be in Buenos Aires on your own if you choose to arrive before embarking or remain after leaving the ship, depending upon your itinerary. Therefore there will be no ship-sponsored tours of the city. To maximize your visit to this outstanding city that is so vital and exciting, there are several ways to get around, all dependent upon your sense of adventure
* The easiest way is to have your hotel arrange a private car with a driver/guide to take you around the city for one or two days, enabling you to visit all of the major sites without any worries about using public transportation or getting lost. If you do not speak Spanish this is the best way to enjoy the city.
* If you stay in the city center, Retiro or Recoleta, you can walk to many important venues from your hotel. Utilizing this book or the

more highly detailed actual guidebooks, you can learn about each important landmark you visit. During the day most parts of Buenos Aires are very safe, comparable to Europe or most of North America. About the only concern in crowded areas would be for pickpockets. At night such locales as Calle Florida, Retiro or Recoleta are safe for pedestrians, as there are large crowds of people.

*The hop on hop off busses are available during the daytime and there are also actual bus tours that your hotel can arrange.

* Public transport within Buenos Aires is facilitated by both a Metro called the SubT, or subway system, and interurban railroad network. There is almost no locale within the metropolitan area that cannot be reached by either metro or commuter train. The city operates a fleet of modern busses that travel down almost every principal street in the city. It is, however, difficult to use these facilities without some working knowledge of Spanish.

* There are also thousands of yellow and black taxicabs that are constantly in motion, as this is a city where people always seem to be on the move.

* Renting a car and trying to see the city on your own is not something I recommend. There is a lot of traffic and local drivers are very aggressive. All signs are written in Spanish and all speeds are shown in kilometers, which for American or British guests can be challenging. And traffic is maddening. Even crossing the street as a pedestrian can pose problems. So be wise and do not rent a car.

In addition to being a dynamic residential and commercial center, remember that Buenos Aires is also the country's capital and center of finance, major seaport, railroad hub and a center of diverse manufacturing. It is this diversity that gives Buenos Aires is importance and has enabled the city to grow to where its population makes it the most significant single locale in the entire nation. Thus it is a very busy and large city, and not only is driving difficult, but parking in the city center can be an impossibility.

EXCURSIONS OUT OF THE CITY: You can arrange for private or group excursions outside of the city through your hotel or the visitor's bureau. The most popular outside excursion is to visit an estancia on the Pampa. Such visits give you a chance to see what life is like for working cowboys or gauchos, and to sample the roasted meats from an asado out of doors. Many estancia owners graciously open their homes and property to visitors, but such visits must be prearranged. If seeing another aspect of Argentine life is something of interest to you, then I highly recommend an estancia visit.

Another one-day excursion that can be done as part of a group or on your own is a visit across the Rio de la Plata to the preserved historic town of Colonia de Sacramento in Uruguay. There are ferryboats and hydrofoils that cross to this beautifully preserved World Heritage Site in about two hours or less. All that is needed is a ticket and your passport. Currency exchange is normally available at the ferryboat terminal or upon arrival in Uruguay. But many restaurants and shops will accept Argentine pesos. Colonia de Sacramento is especially well preserved and gives you the architectural and cultural flavor of life in the early years of settlement.

A visit to Iguaçu Falls on the Argentina Brazil border is not a trip that can be made in a single day. Generally this excursion is available from your cruise line as either a before or after land excursion, for overnight or two nights. Iguaçu Falls is the second largest cataract in the world, and it is breathtaking beyond description. It is a memorable experience that you will keep with you for the rest of your life. The falls consist of numerous cataracts that plunge over an escarpment a mile wide and several hundred feet high. The Rio Paraná is a massive waterway draining south out of the tropical savanna country of Paraguay and Brazil, carrying a vast quantity of water. The Rio Iguaçu is a tributary to the Rio Paraná, and it is here that the falls are located. When the river reaches the escarpment, the water plunges over the edge with tremendous force, causing a thunderous roar that can be heard a couple miles away. And the spray often showers the entire region.

When visiting Iguaçu Falls, you will be required to view the waters only from the Argentine side of the border, as to enter Brazil even to photograph the falls from another perspective requires a visa. If you have a Brazilian visa, then of course you can enter the country to view the falls.

The Argentine city of Porto Iguaçu is located where the Rio Paraná and Rio Iguaçu meet, and it is here that the bridge crossing into Brazil is located. The Brazilian town of Foz do Iguaçu also borders Paraguay across the Rio Paraná where you can cross into Ciudad del Este. I recommend against this without the services of a guide. Ciudad del Este has been a major conduit for drug smuggling and drug enforcement officers often call it the "wild, wild west." It is not the kind of place you would want to visit on your own. If you are like me, you may be tempted to cross just to add another country to your list, but please do not do so unaccompanied.

MAJOR SITES NOT TO MISS: When visiting Buenos Aires, these are the most important venues that you should try and visit above all else:

* Recoleta - The most popular neighborhood in the city, home to great restaurants, exclusive shops, major five-star hotels and many foreign embassies, it is the center of upscale Buenos Aires life.

* Recoleta Cemetery - This is without a doubt the most popular first venue for so many foreign visitors. Not only is the cemetery in the heart of Recoleta fascinating, but most visitors want to simply see the tomb of Eva Peron, no doubt one of the most famous 20th century women in the world. The cemetery is open from 7 AM to 6:30 PM daily.

* Calle Florida - This shopping street in the heart of the city is famous for both its fine quality Argentine leather goods, but equally for its colorful tango dancers who add a definite flavor to the street. A stroll down Calle Florida is a true taste of Buenos Aires.

* San Telmo - One of the most historic colonial districts located south of the city center, San Telmo drips with beautiful colonial charm. And on the weekend, it is noted for its extensive flea market that draws people from all over the city.

* La Boca - South of San Telmo, this old port district, which is the home of Tango, is composed of what are essentially shanties, many built of scrap and sheet iron. But all the buildings are painted in garish colors, some with murals, and they add a distinctive gritty note to this early historic district.

* Avenida 9 de Julio - Stroll down what is probably the widest street in the world, beautifully planted with tall shade trees on its two divider strips. It is lined with buildings from the late 19th and early 20th centuries, giving Buenos Aires its Old World flavor.

* Plaza de Mayo - This is a famous plaza in front of the Casa Rosada, or presidential palace. It was from the balcony of the palace that Juan and Eva Peron used to address the masses. Today political demonstrations are held here whenever there is a need for the public to express its displeasure with the government.

* Puerto Madero - Once the gritty waterfront, today Puerto Madero is one of the most rapidly developing districts. Modern high-rise towers, fashionable hotels, great restaurants and shopping centers have developed amid what were once wharves for shipping, but today house pleasure craft.

* Catedral Metropolitana - Located on Plaza de Mayo, this massive cathedral is home to the principal cardinal for the vast Argentine region. This was once the home church for the cardinal who is today better known as Pope Francis I. It is open weekdays from 7:30 AM to 6:30 PM, weekends from 9 AM to 6:45 PM.

* Museo Nacional de Bellas Artes - Located in Belgrano at Avenida del Liberador 1473, this is a major museum of fine art, including both Old World and Latin American. Open Tuesday thru Friday 11 AM to 8 PM and weekends from 10 AM to 8 PM.

* Teatro Colon - The great opera house of Buenos Aires fronting on Avenida 9 de Julio, but whose address is Calle Cerrito 628, it is a magnificent Old World building. It is best seen if you can attend a performance, but check with your hotel regarding what is playing when you are visiting.

* Retiro Station - The city's main commuter rail station with lines extending north, Retiro Station is a fine example of late 19th century elegance when rail was the only way to travel any distance. The building is beautifully maintained

* Plaza San Martin - Opposite Retiro Station, this is one of the liveliest plazas in the city where it is enjoyable to just sit on a park bench and people watch. You will see quite a cross section of Buenos Aires life. My favorite are the dog walkers, mainly from Recoleta where they are walking up to ten dogs belonging to wealthy clients.

* Jardin Botánico Carlos Thays - Located in Palermo at Avenida del Libertador and Domego y Figueroa Alcorta, this is one of the most elegant and beautiful botanical gardens. In summer it is the coolest and most refreshing place in the city where you can stroll among leafy trees around its beautiful lagoon. It is open daily from 9:30 AM to 6:45 PM.

There are many more specific venues such as small museums, churches, great public buildings and parks, but if I were to list them all, it would represent more than you could see in two or three days. The venues above are the most important and recognizable in the city, giving you a good overview.

DINING OUT: The very first time I went to Buenos Aires, I was worried that I would have to consume large quantities of meat, as we all know that Argentina is one of the world's major beef, lamb and pork producers. And the country has one of the highest per capita consumptions of meat. I was pleasantly surprised to see how much fresh seafood was available, and chicken is also on most restaurant menus. The main form of preparation for meat is to grill it over an open flame produced by using wood. The large fire pit, called the asado, is a fundamental feature of so many Argentine restaurants.

Breakfast is a significant meal in hotels, but at home most Argentinos will have coffee, rolls, some cheese and fruit. This is very similar to breakfast in Europe. But in up market hotels the breakfast buffet is very lavish with smoked meats and fish, cheeses, fruits, a variety of hot or cold cereals, egg dishes and a major selection of breads and pastries. Lunch is served until around three or four in the afternoon, and it can vary depending upon the type of restaurant. Most working Argentino have an empanada, essentially a meat stuffed turnover that is baked or fried. They may have a sandwich, generally with meat filling. In major hotels and restaurants lunch can become your main meal if you are not accustomed to eating at 10 PM, which is the average dinner hour for most Argentinos. Lunch can be quite elegant and commodious. The first course is generally taken from a buffet and consists of many salads, smoked meats and fish, hot beans and rice and other casserole dishes. Then the main course is ordered from a menu and is served by the waiter. This may be meat, fish, seafood or chicken served with all the accompaniments. Finally, if you still have room, most restaurants will have a self-service sweet table with fruits, tortes and pastries. Dinner is essentially a repeat of lunch with the same array of appetizers, main courses and desserts.

There are so many restaurants from which to choose that a list of even the five or six top names will simply be a short guide. And the restaurants I have listed are those that I personally favor, meaning that they have a high standard of excellence and are among the pricier establishments serving traditional Argentine cuisine. If you describe your personal tastes to the hotel concierge, he or she can then tailor recommendations to your taste. Always have the hotel check on the hours of service and be certain to make a reservation, as people generally do not just arrive without having booked a table. But here are my six favorites:
* I Latina - Located at Murilo 725 in suburban Villa Crespo, it will be necessary to take a taxi because it is a few miles west of Recoleta. The restaurant features a special tasting menu that enables you to sample more dishes. The menu combines Argentine dishes with those from other parts of South America. Given its high standards, the prices when converted to U. S. Dollars or Euro are not extreme. Open Tuesday thru Sturday 8 to 11:30 PM. Closed Sunday and Monday.
* Aramburu - This restaurant also features the traditions of Latin America and has a very special 19 course tasting menu as well as regular menu service. The dishes are expertly prepared and serviced in a gracious manner. The restaurant is located at Avenida Salta 1015, just west of Avenida 9 de Julio. A taxi is your best means of reaching the restaurant, as it is just a bit too far from the Retiro and Recoleta hotel district. Open Tuesday thru Saturday 8:30 to 10 PM.

* The Argentine Experience - This restaurant comes very highly rated in Trip Advisor, as it is especially popular with tourists. Not only are the dishes genuine to Argentine gastronomy, but you also learn how to prepare them, adding a bit of entertainment to the meal. For this reason plus the excellent food, it is especially popular. It is located at Avenida Fitzroy 2110 in fashionable Palermo, but still a taxi ride from most major hotels. And it opens at 6:15 PM, knowing that many foreign visitors do not wish to dine after 10 PM.

* Santos Manjares - Here is a very typical Argentine restaurant in which the asado is the featured means of cooking not only the meats and chicken but even the vegetables. At lunch there are hot and tasty empanadas, so traditional. The prices are exceptionally reasonable given the quality. It is located at Avenida Paraguay 938 just east of Avenida 9 de Julio in the heart of the city, and can be reached on foot from most hotels in Retiro or Recoleta. Open Monday thru Saturday from 11:45 AM to 4:30 PM.

* UCO _ This restaurant features both lunch and dinner. It is located in the Fierro Hotel on Avenida Soler in Colegiales, just south of Belgrano. It is not far from Recoleta, but a taxi is needed. The restaurant features many Argentine and other South American dishes and includes a variety of seafood and items such as paella, rabbit and ceviche. It is a small restaurant, very intimate, but impeccable. It is open daily from 7:30 to 11 AM and 12:30 to 11 PM.

* Steaks by Luis - A traditional Argentine asado in which meat is definitely the specialty of the house. But the steaks and chops are all beautifully prepared. Since the portions are large, go easy on the appetizers despite how delicious they are. This restaurant is in Palermo at Jeronimo Salguero #1410. Open Monday, Tuesday, Thursday and Saturday from 8 to 11 PM by reservation only.

If you like ice cream, as most of us do, then you must go to Freddo at Patio Bullrich and taste some of the creamiest and most delectable ice cream you have ever had. They are famous throughout Buenos Aires. And one flavor that is very distinctly Argentine is dulce de leche. This is made with milk that has been cooked with sugar for hours until it becomes a caramelized cream. Dulce de leche is even sold as a spread for toast or muffins and is very popular in Argentina.

SHOPPING: There are numerous fine shopping venues in Buenos Aires. Of all the local products, the most popular is leather. Argentina is one of the world's largest producers of cattle, and leather is used for portfolios, wallets, purses, shoes and coats or jackets. Argentine leather and the craftsmanship going into making finished goods is among the best in the world. The important shopping venues are:

* Calle Florida - The principal shopping street of Buenos Aires, devoted to pedestrians and having a wide array of shops and boutiques.

* Patio Bullrich - Situated in Recoleta across from the Caesar Park Hotel at Posadas 1245. This is a very glamorous multi-level shopping mall without a major anchor store. It is made up of very elegant boutiques and eateries. This is the place for the rich to see and be seen. It is open daily from 10 AM to 9 PM.

* Abasto - This is the largest mall in Buenos Aires, located on Corrientes 3247 adjacent to the Carlos Gardel Station of the SubT. With over 200 shops, it caters to every taste, has a movie theater and large food court. It is open daily from 10 AM to 10 PM/

* Alto Palermo - An older mall that has been recently renovated, Alto Palermo is very heavily laced with brand name shops that tend to favor women rather than men. It is located at Santa Fe and Coronel Diaz in the suburb of Palermo. It is open daily from 10 AM to a0 PM.

* Galeria Pacifico - In the city center on Calle Florida at Córdoba, this mall is favored by foreign visitors because of it being within walking distance to all the major upmarket hotels. It is open daily from 10 AM to 9 PM.

FINAL WORDS: Buenos Aires is a great city, one of world-class stature. So please do yourself a favor and spend a few days to soak up the ambiance and indulge in its good food. You will set yourself off for a great cruise if this is your port of embarkation, and it will be a great way to unwind if you arrive at the end of your cruise. Buenos Aires is not to be missed.

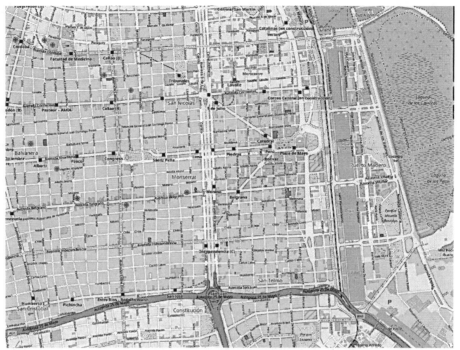

The city center of Buenos Aires l (© OpenStreetMap contributors)

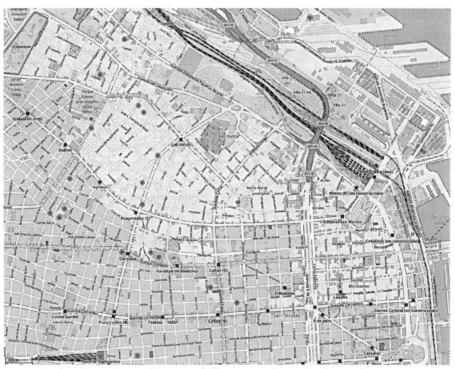

Upscale Recoleta district of Buenos Aires (© OpenStreetMap contributors)

La Boca and San Telmo districts of Buenos Aires. (© OpenStreetMap contributors)

High above Buenos Aires (Work of Fredlyfish4, CC BY SA 4.0 Wikimedia. org CC BY SA2.0).

Avenida Mayo leading to the Congreso (Work of Jorge Royn, Wikimedia.org CC BY SA 3.0)

Avenida Corientes in the city center

The Casa Rosada on Plaza de Mayo

The new Metrobus lanes on Avenida 9 de Julio (Work of Andrezej Otrbski, CC BY SA 4.0, Wikimedia.org)

Tango being performed on Calle Florida

Historic Colonial architecture in San Telmo

Colonial buildings abound in San Telmo

Colorful La Boca is the birthplace of Tango

The dynamic new skyline of Puerto Madero (Work of Stanley Wood, CC BY SA 2.0, Wikimedia.org)

Exclusive high-density living in Recoleta

The Alvear Palace Hotel in Recoleta - one of the finest

One of the dog walkers for wealthy residents of Recoleta

Tourists wandering through Recoleta Cemetery

Busy Avenida Libratador in Belgrano

Avenida Cabildo is the main shopping street of Palermo/Belgrano

The dynamic skyline of Palermo (Work of Martin Terber, CC BY SA 2.0, Wikimedia.org)

VISITING URUGUAY

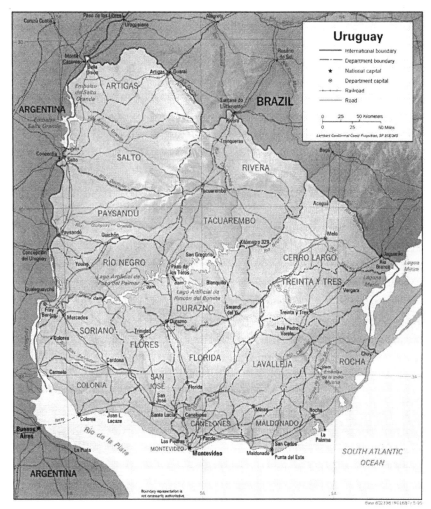

A locational map of Uruguay (© OpenStreetMap contributors)

The vast majority of cruises around the Cone of South America that either leave Buenos Aires or follow an eastbound route from Valparaiso, Chile will include one to two port calls in Uruguay. Montevideo, the national capital and largest city and Punta del Este (Maldonado) are the two ports that major cruise lines will visit.

MONTEVIDEO: The capital and largest city of Montevideo with 1,947,000 people is the nerve center of Uruguay. The city's population equals nearly two thirds of the entire nation, thus making this a country in which its major city is so dominant.

The Portuguese built a fort on the site of the present city in 1723, and one year later an expeditionary force was sent from Buenos Aires to claim this as a Spanish territory, which they easily did. Thus it was Spain that settled and created the outpost of Montevideo that would grow into the modern city. With rich farmland and grazing country to support it, Montevideo quickly became the rival to Buenos Aires across the Rio de la Plata. But conflict between Spain and Portugal and later the political strife that plagued an independent Uruguay kept Montevideo from ever becoming a serious rival.

The city did, however, take on much of the flavor of Buenos Aires, but on a smaller scale. To this day, the city center and its surrounding residential neighborhoods is strongly reflective of the European architectural flavor of Buenos Aires, that being primarily French and Spanish. Like Buenos Aires, the streets in the central city are lined with buildings dating back to the 18th and 19th centuries and they exude a strong degree of Old World elegance. In the port area, the buildings are very reminiscent of the San Telmo district of Buenos Aires, but there is nothing to rival La Boca. Being a smaller city, the extent of the old inner city is that of the small peninsula upon which it is built.

West of the central city peninsula one finds the predominantly blue-collar neighborhoods with smaller, primarily flat roof buildings painted in faded pastel colors. Houses are often hidden behind a plain facade or a wall, but the streets are mostly tree lined. The western suburbs surround the bay that extends inland and was the sheltered anchorage that enticed the Portuguese and later Spanish to develop this as a port. Thus the waterfront is oriented toward manufacturing and shipping and there are no beaches.

East of the central city are the newer suburbs with more sprawling single story houses that very much resemble the so-called "ranch" style popular in the United States. And the predominant building material is red brick. The beach frontage on the eastern shore is lined with fashionable high-rise apartment blocks, making this one of the most sought after parts of Montevideo. And the beaches occur as crescents between rocky headlands, lending an air of beauty to this coastline, similar in its geography to the beaches of Sydney, Australia.

For visitors to Montevideo on a one day port call there are several points of interest that are included on sponsored cruise tours. They can also be blended together to fit individual tastes on privately escorted tours. To simply go off on your own and try to explore beyond the central city is difficult. Montevideo does not have a rapid transit system or Metro. The city is serviced by bus routes, but to get around a working knowledge of Spanish would be required, as visitors generally do not go off on their own since this is not a city well adapted to tourism. The major not to be missed sites include:

* Ciudad Vieja - The old city area that is primarily residential and has been home to port workers and other blue collar employees for the last two centuries. It is also home to the original Jewish synagogue dating to the 19th century.

* Plaza Matriz - Right in the heart of Ciudad Vieja, this plaza is the focal point of the old city. Often there is either a flea market or craft market in the plaza, especially on days when a ship is in port.

* Plaza Independencia - Here is the main plaza in the center of the city, surrounded by the major skyscrapers, primarily built in the early to mid 20th century. Often various civic functions are held in the Plaza.

* Palacio Salvo - The tallest building in Montevideo, this is a classic early 20th century example of Art Decó design, similar in flavor to the older architecture of Buenos Aires, and it was once the tallest building on the continent. You can visit daily between 10:30 AM and 4 PM and on Wednesday night from 8 to 9:30 PM.

* Torre de Comunicaciones - Located along the top end of the harbor, the view from the public observation deck on the 24th floor is sensational on a clear day. However, unless your group tour stops here, or you have a private car and driver, do not attempt to go on your own because you will loose valuable time. Visits of under 10 allowed Monday, Wednesday, Friday from 3:30 to 5 PM and Monday and Tuesday from 10:30 AM to Noon. Call for reservations.

* Catedral Matriz - Built in 1804, this is the city's main center of Catholic worship and also is the burial place of the most prominent of citizens. It is open daily but no specific opening or closing hours are given.

* Positos along La Rambla - This beautiful beachfront walkway is similar in flavor to Copacabana in Rio de Janeiro, but unlike Rio there is little worry about becoming a victim of petty crime. La Rambla runs for several miles from the edge of the city center into Positos, the most sought after suburb.

Palacio Legislativo - The neo-Classical 19th century parliament building on the northern edge of the city center is the center for the Uruguayan government. Tours given in Spanish or Portuguese daily at 10:30 AM and English at 3 PM daily

* Mercado Agricola Montevideo - A large public market that features the great abundance of food produced in the surrounding countryside. The market is located at Jose L. Terra 2220, and you would either need

to have it on your tour itinerary or if you were out privately, your driver or a taxi will know its location. Open daily from 2 AM to 10 PM.

* Parque Rodo - A beautiful seaside park that is also a center for dining and nightlife.

* Plaza Fabini - This is a beautiful central city plaza and often hosts local artisans.

* Parque Prado - The city's largest park located in the western suburbs. It is home to the botanical garden, many sports venues and also an imposing statue dedicated to the former indigenous people who once inhabited Uruguay, but who were all decimated.

* Teatro Solis - This Romanesque building is the city's primary opera house and concert hall, located at Calle Buenos Aires 652 in the city center and you may be able to attend a matinee performance if one is scheduled on the day you are in Montevideo.

* Auditorio Sodre - This active theater with a magnificent interior has a major program of music, ballet and drama throughout the year. However as a one-day visitor all you can hope to do is peak inside unless a matinee is held the day you are in Montevideo.

The most enjoyable way to get outside of the city if that is your preference is to take a group tour to one of the wineries located north of the city. The drive into the countryside is quite pleasant, and a wine tasting can be quite enjoyable. Most of the tours to the wineries offer not only a sampling of the wines, but usually include a tango show and refreshments such as warm empanadas, which can be quite filling as well as delicious.

DINING OUT: If you are on an all day tour of Montevideo, lunch will be provided at a nice restaurant, but the cruise line will have prearranged it. If you are traveling around the city with a private car and driver/guide, or if you are walking in the central city, you will have a choice for lunch. The few restaurants I have listed below are my recommendations for a nice lunch with a taste of Uruguay:

* Bouza Bodega Boutique - Located well out of the city to the northwest on Camino de La Redencion 7658, it is only practical to go if you have a private car, as a taxi ride each way will be expensive. This is a superb venue for traditional asado, with meat and good wine being the specialty. Open Monday thru Saturday 9 AM to 7 PM.

* WASA Ethnik Food - Here is one of the few excellent restaurants in the city center that is open for lunch, but not dinner. Its hours are 11:30 AM to 4 PM. The food is sensational and it has a very wide range of ethnic choices just as the name implies. It is located at Calle Zabala

1341 not far from the metropolitan cathedral area, walking distance from Plaza Independencia.

* Es Mercat - Here is a good seafood restaurant that is open from morning until 5:30 PM and dinner until 11 PM daily. It is in a somewhat shabby neighborhood, but it is very popular with locals. Located at Avenida Colón 1550, it is not far from the cruise terminal. Do not be put off by the neighborhood. The restaurant is top quality.

* Doña Ines Dulces Tentaciones - If you can translate Spanish, you will see that this is a place for light lunches, but primarily for sweet temptations. Located at Miguel Barreiro 3293, this small cafe serves great sandwiches and very tempting homemade desserts along with a variety of teas and coffees. The location is right in the heart of Playa de los Positos, one of the cities best-loved beach areas. Open from 2 to 8 PM Saturday, Monday and Tuesday, 8AM to 1 PM Wednesday thru Friday.

SHOPPING: On a one day visit, you will have little time for shopping if it is the city that you want to see. However, if you do have some time left over, the main shopping street is Avenida 8 de Julio, extending northeast from the Plaza Independencia. Here you will find fashionable leather clothing, a specialty of Uruguay just as it is in Argentina. In the Plaza Matriz you may find a craft market, and one item that represents fine Uruguayo craftsmanship is the handmade wood box or small chest. The woodworkers are noted for their fine skill at marquetry, that is the inlay of different woods to create a specific design.

PUNTA DEL ESTE: Located about 80 miles east along the coast are the cities of Maldonado and Punta del Este, the most popular beach resort in Uruguay. Maldonado is the older city, dating to 1755. It has around 63,000 residents, including several satellite towns strung out along the beach. In the central area of Maldonado you will see a more traditional view of Uruguay both with regard to beautiful colonial and post-colonial architecture and a quiet way of life so typical of the smaller cities and towns of the country. This stands in stark contrast with its neighbor Punta del Este. In 1957, it was declared a city, as its resort development had taken root. In 1967, it hosted the American Summit. And in 1986, it played host to the first of several conferences that led to the creation of the World Trade Organization.

Punta Ballena, Laguna del Diario and Los Ceibos, which are popular beach communities are all a part of greater Maldonado.

Punta del Este occupies a small peninsula of land that juts out into the sea, and it its northern residential district merges with Maldonado. It only has a population of approximately 10,000 full time residents, but its many high-rise apartments give the impression of a more populated community. But it does register nearly 24,000 households. Understandably as a major resort, most of the apartments and many of the single-family homes are owned by foreigners from either Argentina or Brazil. These are second homes that are occupied only part-time. Punta del Este began with a botanical garden in 1896, and by 1907 there was a small town chartered.

Punta del Este is also a major center for high end shopping, as being a resort for the rich; the shops cater to high fashion, jewelry and other accessories. There are also numerous high end restaurants and bistros located in this small community. Focal to the heart of Punta del Este is the high rise Conrad Hotel and Casino and the Avenida Gorlero shopping district.

This is a major center for recreation and retirement greatly favored by Argentinos and Brazilians because of its high sense of fashion and style and also its miles of white sand. Cruise visits are now a part of most cruises between Buenos Aires and Valparaiso, but unfortunately there are no docking facilities for anything other than very small private craft. This requires what is called a tender stop. The ship anchors offshore usually about two to three miles. Generally two to four lifeboats are lowered, depending upon the size of the ship, and from a floating pontoon you board the tender for the short ride into the yacht harbor of Punta del Este. You need to plan your day because it can take up to an hour to get to shore depending upon how many people wish to tender at a given time. On smaller more up market cruise ships, you may only need to allow around 20 minutes to and from shore, but it is still not as easy as just stepping down the gangway.

There are not a lot of specific visitor attractions in Punta del Este or Maldonado. The main focus is to simply enjoy walking around the heart of Punta del Este, soaking in the ambiance and people watching. Among those specific sites that are of interest for a one-day visit you will find:
* Casapueblo - A very architecturally distinct hotel built down the side of a cliff overlooking the sea. It is located in Punta Ballena just a few miles outside of central Punta del Este. If a tour is offered by your ship, it is well worth taking.

* Puerto del Este - This is the yacht harbor where your ship's tender will dock, and it is filled with cafes and shops.
* Arboretum Lussich - A beautiful garden overlooking the sea, but you either need to be on a tour that includes a stop or take a local taxi, which is safe to do. It is open from 10 AM to 6:30 PM daily.
San Fernando de Maldonado Cathedral - This is the main cathedral in the heart of old Maldonado. It is open daily but no hours are given.
* Puente Lionel Vieira - Located in La Barra, this is a rather unique bridge that appears over the water as two waves. It is architecturally unique.

DINING OUT: One must while in Punta del Este is to have lunch at one of the many waterfront restaurants. Seafood is naturally the prime ingredient. But apart from the fresh seafood, the views along the beach and out over the water combined with people watching make this a very special stop. As noted before, ambiance is very much a part of spending your day in Punta del Este, the premier beach resort for people from Buenos Aires, Argentina all the way north to São Paulo, Brazil.

Of the many restaurants along the waterfront on the west side of the peninsula, most are not open for lunch. Most of the restaurants offer Italian, French and Mediterranean cuisine. Remember this is a resort that caters to local Argentino and Brazilian clients, so traditional Uruguayo cuisine is not what they want. Of those that that offer traditional local cuisine or unique desserts and snacks, I recommend the following:
* Virazon - One of the few major restaurants open at lunch and serving seafood in a variety of ways typical to South America. It is not overly grand, but it is spacious and right on the beach and popular with locals. Located along Rambla Portuaria at Calle 18. It is open daily from 8 AM until 3 AM.
* Churros Manolo - A churro is a fried dessert pastry popular throughout the Spanish countries of South America. But here the churros are filled with dulce de leche and are a melt in your mouth snack. This take out cafe is downtown at Calle 29 and Avenida Gorlero. It is open from 4:30 PM until 2 AM daily.
* Tea for Three - A small cafe serving sandwiches and light fare, but well known locally for its delectable and rich desserts. Located at Gallerias Open Mall, it is a favorite. It is open from 10 AM to 8 PM Tuesday thru Saturday.
* Freddo - The venerable Buenos Aires ice cream shop at Avenida Gorlero and Calle 27 is a household institution among locals, and

rightly so. Open daily from 10 AM to 11 PM, extended to Midnight Friday thru Sunday.

SHOPPING: There are a few shops along Avenida Gorlero that sell traditional Uruguayo arts and crafts, but nothing different from what you might have seen in Montevideo, or will see if your cruise stops in Punta del Este first. However, there is a very good traditional arts shop/gallery inside the Conrad Hotel that I would recommend. The majority of the shops along Avenida Gorlero are oriented toward wealthy Argentino or Brazilian summer visitors who will buy expensive jewelry or casual clothing while on vacation.

FINAL WORDS: Some cruise itineraries skip a visit to Uruguay, which is a shame because this is one of the most idyllic countries in South America. And Montevideo and Punta del Este are very enjoyable stops. Likewise some cruise itineraries skip the next destination in this book - the Falkland Islands.

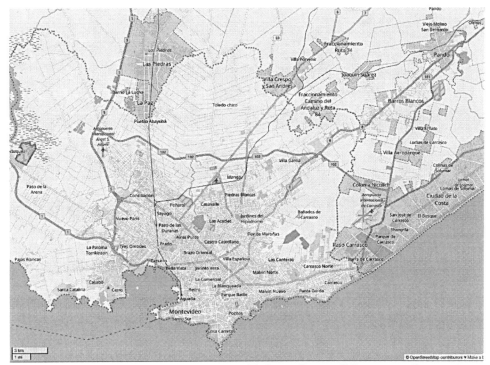

A map of Montevideo, Uruguay (©OpenStreet Map contributors)

A map of central Montevideo (©OpenStreet Map contributors)

An aerial view over the city center of Montevideo

An aerial view of the city of Montevideo to the left of the view above

Independence Square in the heart of Montevideo

In Old Town Montevideo

The Parliament of Uruguay

In the westside barrio of Montevideo

Positos Beach is one of the most upscale parts of Montevideo

Colorful flowers growing in Positos

Modern suburbia in Montevideo

A map of greater Maldonado (© OpenStreetMap contributors)

A map of Punta del Este (© OpenStreetMap contributors)

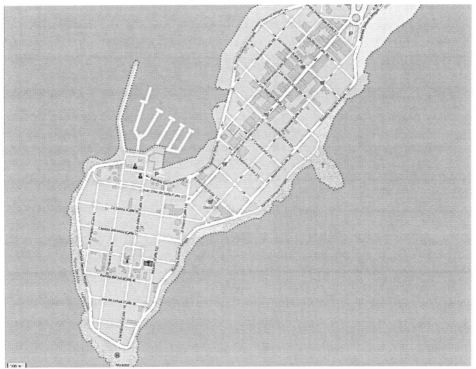

A map of central Punta del Este (© OpenStreetMap contributors)

The Punta del Este skyline

The large Punta del Este private yacht harbor

The sweep of the beachfront in Punta del Este

The white sandy beaches of Punta del Este

Avenida Gorlero, the main high end shopping street in Punta del Este

Massive high-rise development in Punta del Este

The elegance of condo living in Punta del Este

Life is good and people enjoy the out of doors

THE PATAGONIA COAST

Depending upon whether you are traveling to or from Buenos Aires, it appears that only about half of all cruise itineraries among the major cruise lines include a port call along the coast of Patagonia in Argentina. And that port is Puerto Madryn, a rather jaunty little city with a fair degree of urban sophistication.

Patagonia is a vast region that stretches from the southern margins of the Pampas all the way to the Straits of Magellan, about 40 percent of the length of Argentina. Most of Patagonia consists of a broken plain that dips eastward from the Andes to the South Atlantic Ocean. Cold westerly winds blow off the snow and glacier covered peaks and whip across the short grasses of Patagonia, stirring clouds of dust and penetrating the bodies of man and beast alike. In comparison to any portions of North America, Patagonia can best be compared to the dry high plains of eastern Montana and Wyoming. There are fewer people than in the American high plains states simply because this southern tail of Argentina is land's end for the continent. From the crest of the Andes, which form the border with Chile, it is only an average distance of 350 kilometers or 250 miles to the South Atlantic Ocean, and to compound matters, there are few deep-water anchorages along this entire coast.

This is rather cold and bleak short grassland unlike the moderate tall grass Pampas or the humid tropical Gran Chaco in the far north of Argentina. The continent begins to narrow south of Buenos Aires to where there is less land between the high Andes Mountains along the border with Chile and the South Atlantic Ocean. The prevailing wind in these middle latitudes blow regularly from the west, tracking winter storms against the Chilean coast and the Andes. This leaves little moisture to crest the mountains and bring precipitation to Patagonia. Thus the region has developed since the end of the last ice age as a steppe, or semi-arid short grassland. Winds blowing off the mountains are generally cold and rainfall or snow is scant. It is a hard region in which to live, yet hardy settlers have managed to find that they can raise sheep and prosper. Ranches are large in area, but carrying capacity is low. Towns are few and far apart, mainly along the coast where fishing provides for an alternate way of living. In more recent decades, small quantities of oil and natural gas have added to the local economy. And a small amount of tourism has augmented the local economy. Visitors come to enjoy the marine life along the shores - whales, seals and penguins in particular.

The mountain slopes, however, are lush and green, as they receive significant snowfall and summer rain, but the effect is quickly lost once leaving the mountains. This region contains a mix of young volcanic cones whose peaks rise to 3,660 meters or 12,000 feet combined with uplifted crags whose heights can 4,572 meters or 15,000 feet toward the northern edge of the region. Of course, farther north into the central Andean region, mountain peaks can top 6,096 meters or 20,000 feet. The mountains in the Patagonia region were heavily glaciated during the four ice advances of the Pleistocene, and today there are still active glaciers in the most southerly margins of both Argentina and Chile. The remnant lakes formed during the Pleistocene are one of this region's most noted features, providing both Argentina and Chile with magnificent, cold lakes in a variety of sizes. This has created a vacation paradise for both countries and is collectively known as the Lakes District. Some of the lakes actually fill valleys that were carved out between the high peaks and straddle the border between the two nations. Thick forests of southern beech and other hardwoods mingle with planted forests of pine and fir, brought by early settlers.

Inland visitors come to marvel and the magnificent glaciers that have pushed eastward from the South Patagonian Ice Field. The scenery is rather stark, but breathtaking and those visitors who truly crave an outdoor adventure are richly rewarded.

SETTLEMENT: It was the German, Welsh and Scottish immigrants to Argentina that chose this region, as it reminded them so much of home. They established large ranches to raise sheep and some cattle that thrive on the rich grasses close to the mountains, but only dairy cattle can truly prosper in this cold region. And the timber industry was once quite active, but today tourism dominates the Lakes District where the majority of settlement occurred. Most of the tourist activity is found in the northern reaches of the Patagonian Andes, centering on San Carlos de Bariloche. This popular city, simply known as Bariloche, is the number one resort destination in the interior of Argentina and it rivals Mar del Plata for the attention of foreign visitors. However, when it comes to scenic potential, there is no equal. The region around Bariloche is one of the most beautiful of mountain environments to be found anywhere in the entire world. And what adds to its beauty is the pristine nature of the region. There has been little deforestation or development, enabling the visitor to see what amounts to raw, unspoiled wilderness, yet with all of the comforts that modern 21st century life can provide.

Bariloche is located on the southern shore of Nahuel Huapi Lake, tucked into a valley between high peaks. It is only two hours from Buenos Aires by direct flights, but if you were to travel by car, it would be a journey of nearly three days. Many do motor here during the summer, as it gives people a chance to cross the windswept plains of Patagonia, an experience similar to that many eastern Americans would get if they drove to Yellowstone or Grand Teton National Parks. For cruise ship visitors, a trip by air to Bariloche would be the only logical means of transport, and this could be done as a pre or post cruise excursion, one I highly recommend to anyone who loves spectacular mountain scenery. There are numerous daily flights between Buenos Aires and Bariloche.

HISTORY: This mountainous region and the vast plains of Patagonia were the last portions of Argentina to be settled. The hunting and gathering tribes who inhabited the windswept plains and the more settled lakeside dwelling peoples resisted Spanish intrusions into their lands until the mid 19th century. Today there are only a handful of native peoples living in scattered villages along the edge of the mountains. As noted, most of the immigrants who chose to come to Patagonia were from central Europe, primarily German, followed by Scottish and Welsh from the British Isles. These hearty immigrants were accustomed to cold weather and blustery conditions, and this region had reminders of home. Bariloche itself was founded in 1902, but Carlos Wiederhold built the first general store in 1895 on the site that would become the town. The name San Carlos de Bariloche honors both the founder and takes its name from an Indian word "vuriloche." The most notorious residents for a brief period were the American outlaws known as "Butch" Cassidy and the "Sundance Kid,' who had a ranch in the general vicinity of Bariloche before moving to Bolivia where it believed they were killed in a bank robbery. During the early 20th century, U. S. President Theodore Roosevelt visited as did other notables all seeking the beauty and wild country of the Andes. By the 1920's, adventurous tourists could fly out from Buenos Aires, and the resort has just continued to grow ever since. Argentina would be so pleased to host the winter Olympic games in Bariloche, however, the reversal of seasons will preclude such a possibility unless the various winter sports federations in the Northern Hemisphere have a change of heart.

The Argentine government has recognized the scenic potential and environmental significance of the Lake District and the southern Andes. As a result, numerous national parks have been created, roads have been built and the tourist infrastructure has been developed. However, the region still is remote to the rest of the country, Bariloche itself being over 1,000 air miles from Buenos Aires. The southernmost sections of Patagonia are still 500 to 1,000 miles farther south than Bariloche.

PUERTO MADRYN: The city of Puerto Madryn is located on the large and sheltered Golfo Nuevo, roughly 805 kilometers or 500 air miles south of Buenos Aires. Its population is only 75,000, yet it gives the feeling of being in a much larger city because it has become the focal commercial center of such a vast ranching and oil-drilling region despite the exceptionally low population density. Welsh immigrants founded the city in 1865 when 100 colonists chose to settle and establish a community, primarily based upon sheep ranching.

The Golfo Nuevo is sheltered from the often-stormy waters of the South Atlantic by the Peninsula Valdeś. It is this peninsula that has drawn many visitors to Puerto Madryn because it is a wildlife sanctuary. Sea lions, fur seals and elephant seals, Magellanic penguins, guanaco, and Argentine grey fox are among the numerous species found on the land or along its shores. And in the waters offshore the southern right whale is seen between May and December, as these are their favored waters for mating and birthing. Orcas also on occasion will lunge ashore when in pursuit of a seal, their favorite meal. Full day tours out of Puerto Madryn give visitors a rare opportunity to enjoy these species that live in a totally undisturbed environment. In 1999, UNESCO extended World Heritage Site status to the peninsula, and the Argentine government is very proud to be maintaining this as a protected reserve. The few cruise itineraries that stop in Puerto Madryn do so primarily to offer various tours into the Peninsula Valdeś for wildlife watching.

Puerto Madryn itself has become a very popular summertime beach resort for Argentinos who do not want to be part of the crowd at Mar de Plata or on the beaches of Chile or Uruguay. Many new condominiums and beachfront homes have been built in Puerto Madryn as second homes for wealthy Porteños who find it quieter and more relaxing than Punta del Este. The result has been to help develop the city of Puerto Madryn into a very fashionable shopping and dining center, its main streets having a measure of sophistication that would otherwise not exist.

If you choose to venture out on your own, there are plenty of local taxis available for hire and many drivers do speak some English. The recommended individual sites include:

* Punta Tombo - Located about one hour outside of the city, this is one of the best locations to see a colony of Magellanic penguins
* El Doradillo Beach - Also at a distance of some 30 miles from the city, this is a prime location between December and May to watch the southern right whale
* Loberia de Punta Loma - A large sea lion colony just about 25 minutes drive from the city center
* Lobo Larsen - Here is a site where operators provide snorkeling equipment and you can swim with sea lions - quite an adventure
* Museo Provincial de Ciencias Naturales y Oceanographico - Located right in the city at Domencq Garcia and Jose Menendez, walking distance from the city center. This museum has excellent exhibits and also a tower from which you can view much of the Golfo Nuevo. The museum is open from 9 AM to 3 PM weekdays, from 3 to 7 PM and closed Sunday.
* Museo de Gemas - This small museum of gems is quite distinctive, and it is especially interesting for anyone interested in semi-precious stones. It also has an excellent collection of the containers and straws used for drinking yerba mate. It is a short distance from the city center, located at Calle San Luis 805. It is open Monday thru Saturday from 9 AM to 12:30 PM and again from 3:30 to 7 PM, closed on Sunday.

If you choose to remain in Puerto Madryn, most cruise lines offer a shuttle bus into the city center. Surprisingly it offers a very distinct urban feel despite the small population. There are several excellent clothing shops, many offering fine quality Argentine leather goods at prices far below those found in Buenos Aires.

DINING OPTIONS: Surprisingly there are some excellent dining establishments in Puerto Madryn, but the majority are only open for dinner, well after the cruise ship will have departed. But of those open for lunch, I highly recommend one establishment where there is consistently good food:
* Panacea - This is a small, but good restaurant that serves a varied menu at lunch. The food is fresh and well prepared. They specialize in both seafood and vegetarian dishes, but with a distinct Argentine flavor. It is a short distance from the city center at Avenida Roca and Apeleg. It is open daily from 7:30 AM until 1 AM.

SHOPPING: There are a few shopping venues worthy of note:
* Yenelen Chocolate - This is a superb chocolate factory and shop that offers a variety of chocolates all prepared in the Bavarian manner. They are open Monday thru Saturday from 9 AM to 8 PM and closed Sunday.
* El Portal de Madryn - A small, but interesting shopping mall in the city center located at Avenida Roca and Avenida 28 de Julio. It is home to several shops with very good clothing, chocolate and local handcrafts. They are open daily from 10 AM to 10 PM.
* Patagonia Rebelde - Located at Avenida Roca 369, this shop features a wide array of local handcraft items. No business hours are listed.

FINAL WORDS: Along the coast some 350 air miles southeast of Bariloche is the small city of Comodoro Rivadada, located on Golfo San Jose. This small port city is now the center of a minor oil-drilling boom. Limited quantities of oil have been found, bringing newfound prosperity to this isolated region.

South of Comodoro Rivadavia there is virtually no development. The isolated main road leads to the last mainland port of Rio Gallegos, located over 1,280 miles south of Buenos Aires. It is the provincial capital of the vast province of Santa Cruz, but its primary role is in the refining of petrochemicals from the oil found in the province. It is also an important naval base, as Argentina has still not forgotten the Falkland Island War and they jealously guard their southern waters. Likewise, the important Straits of Magellan begin 50 miles south of Rio Gallegos. This is a major waterway used by many nations with ships too large to transit the Panama Canal, or by ships carrying goods between east and west coast ports within South America. Thus a military presence is understandable. The only visitors who come this far south are those who want to visit the southern Andean glacial fields, but the vast majority do so on the Chileno side of the border.

Cruise ships do not stop at ports along this southern coast because of the lack of infrastructure, not as a result of the landscape lacking in any beauty. Inland a short ways are glaciers, blue lakes and the looming Andes on the horizon. But despite bypassing these far southern shores, cruise ships do make the journey through the Straits of Magellan, stopping at Punta Arenas, Chile and proceeding across the straits to the island of Tierra del Fuego, visiting Ushuaia, Argentina and, weather permitting, Cape Horn - land's end of the Americas.

A map of Puerto Madryn (© OpenStreetMap contributors)

A map of central Puerto Madryn (© OpenStreetMap contributors)

Looking over Puerto Madryn from the nearby plateau

Along Avenida Roca in the heart of the city

There is a slower pace to life in Puerto Madryn

Investment from Buenos Aires in vacation homes

There is a large tidal range on the gulf seen here at low tide

One of the major seal colonies north of the city on the edge of the peninsula

THE FALKLAND ISLANDS

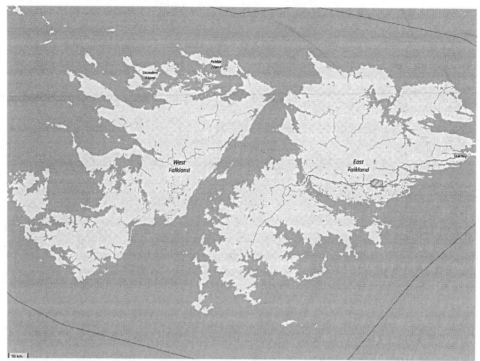

Map of the Falkland Islands (© OpenStreetMap contributors)

It appears that the majority of the cruise lines include a port call in Stanley, Falkland Islands between Buenos Aires and Tierra del Fuego. Only around half of the itineraries follow the coastline of Argentina, stopping at Puerto Madryn in place of visiting the Falkland Islands. This is of course a shorter route and one that can essentially be guaranteed. But whether you will set foot on the Falkland Islands is subject to the whim of the elements. Any itinerary you choose that includes the Falkland Islands is subject to three scenarios:

* Your ship will make the port call without incident, but perhaps the waters en route to the islands and then outbound may be quite choppy.
* Your ship will make the port call, but under extremely poor conditions with very choppy waters showing swells of over ten feet and winds of over 30 miles per hour
* Your ship will have to miss the port call at Stanley because of exceptionally high seas and strong winds , which happens quite often.

In my years of experience with cruising in this part of the world, I have found that a visit to Stanley is generally about a 50/50 occasion. So be prepared for the port call to be cancelled because of weather half of the times.

WHAT TO DO ABOUT BECOMING SEASICK: Despite having stabilizers, the ocean can become rough to the degree where strong pitching or rolling motion will still be felt. And worst of all is the combination of these two motions, which can occur when the ship must travel counter to the flow of the waves so that they are hitting the vessel broadside. If your trip to the Falkland Islands should become more than you had expected, and you begin to feel sick, there are ways in which you can be helped. These include:
* If you anticipate becoming sick, taking an oral or injectable medication to counter the nausea and other symptoms of seasickness. As an alternative, there are patches you can wear that will also distribute the medication over a longer period.
* Do not lie in bed because being in a supine position can only make you feel worse.
* Looking out the window and focusing upon the horizon can help in easing the symptoms.
* Breathing some fresh air also helps, providing it is not too rough where passengers have been told not to go out on deck.
* Eating some dry toast or saltine crackers and drinking hot tea are very helpful, as they help your stomach to not accumulate acids.
* Staying calm and keeping occupied will also help take your mind off the sensation of motion.

THE ISLANDS: The Falkland Islands are a small archipelago located 300 miles off the coast of Argentina's Patagonia at 52 degrees south latitude. The two large islands plus dozens of smaller ones occupy a total land area of 12,172 square kilometers or 4,700 square miles. And the population is just slightly under 3,000. The Falkland Islands are a British Crown Colony, but essentially self-governing. For protection, the British Royal Air Force does maintain a strategic base in the Falklands, important now because Argentina still lays claim to them as Islas Malvinas. Even after a disastrous war with the United Kingdom in 1982 when Argentine forces invaded and occupied the island chain, they persist in claiming "Islas Malvinas Son Argentinas," translated to say the Malvinas Islands belong to Argentina.

The Falkland Islands are quite mountainous or hilly at the least. The0re are few areas of level land. They are of continental origin, a leftover from the distant breakup of the great supercontinent. There are no volcanoes on the Falklands and earthquakes are relatively rare.

Climatically the islands have a cold, wet marine climate with abundant rainfall, some snow, but with wind as the predominant factor. The island chain is essentially treeless because of the gale force winds that do blow across them, especially in winter. This is essentially considered to be a sub Antarctic climate. There are dwarfed shrubs in sheltered areas, and the predominant vegetation is grass. This has encouraged the raising of sheep that thrive in this type of environment similar to that of northern Scotland's Orkney Islands.

The animal life is limited to introduced reindeer, rabbits, pigs and horses. Among the few native animals is the Patagonian fox. But the waters surrounding the Falkland Islands are rich in fur seals, whales and penguins. There are numerous penguin colonies on the shores of the Falklands, a delight to visitors and a major tourist attraction.

You may ask the question, "If the islands are so difficult to always be sure of landing, and if they are not all that scenic, then why go?" It is a valid question. My answer as a geographer is simply, "Because they are there!" What I mean to say is that here in the middle of the South Atlantic Ocean is a group of rocky, somewhat forbidding islands that simply by their existence cry out to be visited. It's not everyone who can return home and say, "I've been to the Falkland Islands."

A BRIEF HISTORY: The first recorded European landing was by the British in 1690. In 1764 and 1766, the French and British established small bases on the island chain. But the French ceded their claim to Spain in 1766 and ultimately the Spanish attempted to wrest the British port away, but soon relented. The British and Spanish coexisted until 1774 when the British gave up their colony on economic grounds, but left a plaque, laying claim to the area in the name of the Crown.

Spain remained as the sole occupant, governing the islands out of Buenos Aires, using them as a penal colony. But with the British militarily active in the Rio de la Plata during the Napoleonic Wars, the Spanish abandoned the islands in 1811.

For the next decade only fishermen would occasionally visit the islands. But the government in Buenos Aires did continue to lay claim to the archipelago. The newly independent Argentina granted a German settler the right to establish a small colony, bringing in other pioneers, but in 1831, a dispute with the Americans over whaling rights caused the USS Lexington to raid the colony and declare its political status neutralized.

In 1832, Argentina reasserted its claim, but the British arrived after a mutiny among Argentine officers. The British reasserted their original claim and it is here that the dispute began to fester. The British did not follow through with military protection for its few settlers and Argentine gauchos returned and attempted to capture the British colonists. It was not until 1840, that the British once again stationed troops on the islands, and declared the Falklands a Crown Colony. Why you might ask. These islands are bleak and have hardly anything to offer, so why did the British show a contempt for the Argentine and attempt to assert themselves on such essentially worthless land. It was simply a matter of national pride, but there was also the strategic value of its southern location with regard both to whaling and to the British maintaining a presence in that part of the world.

During both World Wars, the British did maintain a naval presence in the Falklands, which only further angered Argentina. The British did enter into long-term sovereignty negotiations with Argentina over the islands, but final approval would have to rest with the locals who flatly opposed the idea. Thus negotiations ceased. By 1981, the Thatcher government wanted to divest itself of these islands that do not economically pay for themselves, but local opposition was strong. And in 1982 Argentine forces launched a surprise attack and quick takeover. On principle, the British could not let this stand and they sent a strong naval and marine force that quickly retook the islands. Today fishing disputes and general animosity over the fate of the islands have tainted relations between the two countries. Most recently the British said they would not enter into any further negotiations in that the islands are and will remain British. Yet Argentine sentiment still considers the islands to be theirs, based on so little other than emotion. Even the national weather news includes Islas Malvinas every night, as if they were a part of Argentina.

LIVES OF THE RESIDENTS: If your ship is scheduled to visit the Falkland Islands and weather permits such a port call, you will land in Port Stanley, capital and the only significant town in the colony. This is a surprisingly prosperous colony with very low unemployment, equally low inflation and a high living standard. The mainstay has been fine quality wool and fishing. But today oil exploration and development combined with tourism dominate. With such a tiny population, the islands can prosper with what amounts to one of the world's smallest economies.

Port Stanley is in effect a village. Its neat wood houses line the few streets of the town, and there have been a few trees planted. There is a strong Welsh and Scottish flavor to the community, as the majority of settlers came from those two parts of Great Britain where they were familiar with rugged, windswept landscapes. The town population is 2,121 out of the less than 3,000 who inhabit the whole archipelago. Apart from being self-governing, the islands mint their own currency, which is the Falkland Island Pound, set at the same rate as the British Pound. And they also print their own postage stamps, highly favored among collectors. The residents of the Falkland Islands are considered to be British Subjects and carry full national citizenship.

The elected Legislative Assembly is the main body of government for the islands. The head of state is of course Her Majesty Queen Elizabeth II, but the appointed Governor represents her, and in turn appoints the Chief Executive officer to work with the council. What would amount to a cabinet is composed of the Governor, the Chief Executive and the Director of Finance. The islands function under English Common Law, the Foreign and Commonwealth Office in London oversees their actions. There is a small Royal Falkland Islands Police, and since the 1982 war with Argentina, there is a small light infantry company.

What is there to see in Port Stanley? It is very easy to walk around the town, and most cruise lines do offer a half day tour around the bleak and windswept island, visiting penguin and seal colonies and some tours stopping at a local sheep ranch. In town the sights of interest include:
* 1982 Liberation Memorial - This monument commemorates the Falkland Island War that secured the island's Crown Colony status.
* Falkland Islands Museum - The history and geography of these remote islands are featured in this all important museum that should not be missed. It is open from 10 AM to 4 PM Tuesday thru Friday, and from 2 to 5 PM on weekends. Closed on Monday.
* Christ Church Cathedral - Situated in the heart of town this is the island's main Anglican house of worship and will remind you of a village church in rural England or Scotland. It is the southernmost Anglican Cathedral in the world. No opening hours are posted.
* Museum Britannia House - Located on the edge of Stanley, this small museum is filled with the artifacts and photos of the history of the Falkland Islands. No hours are posted, but they are always open when a ship is in port.
* Victory Green - The main town commons and largest green space in Stanley is the center of Stanley.

* Gypsy Cove - Just outside of Stanley, the cove has a broad sandy beach and is also home to a sizable penguin colony that is often included on any group island tour, but can be accessed by the local taxi, which is a 4x4 vehicle.
* Adventure Falklands Tour - If you choose to not go on one of the ship's organized tours, you can book ahead to this company by writing to them in Stanley. No address is required. They offer a variety of tours to visit various penguin colonies around the main East Falkland Island.

DINING OUT: You will only be in Stanley for lunch, and the choices are quite limited, and relatively expensive, but you must remember where you are. The choices include:
* Malvina House Hotel - Being the major hotel in Stanley, located at 8 Ross Road, its dining room is probably the most versatile on the island. It offers a variety of entrees, but of course fresh fish and lamb are most commonplace. Breakfast is served from 7 to 9:30 AM, lunch from Noon to 1:30 PM and dinner from 7 to 9 PM daily. Sunday a light menu is served from Non to 8 PM.
* Waterfront Cafe - A small cafe on Ross Road in town, serving fresh fish, delicious cakes and coffee or tea. Open daily, but specific hours are not posted.
* Bittersweet - At 58 St. John Street, this small restaurant provides home cooked food in a nice atmosphere. Business hours are not listed.

SHOPPING: You will not find much to buy in Stanley, though there may be a few items of interest, including:
* Falkland Island postage stamps are a valued item among those who collect stamps.
* Wool clothing - There are a few shops selling wool sweaters and jackets, but the majority have either a penguin or the seal of the Falkland Islands, and not all are actually produced on the islands.

FINAL WORDS: If you are fortunate enough to make it to the Falkland Islands, please remember that these are sub Antarctic bleak islands located in an area of extensive wind and storms. The islands are not of volcanic origin, therefore there are no major mountains to be seen. Penguins dominate the wildlife, and over half a million sheep roam their grassy plains. So do not expect to see a lot of historic sites or cultural landmarks. You are in a remote part of the world and it is somewhat of an adventure just being here.

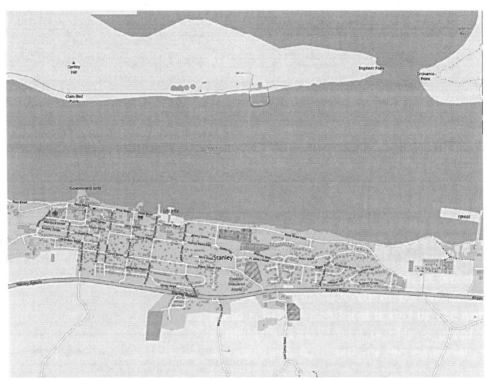

Port Stanley street map (© OpenStreetMap contributors)

The bleak tundra landscape of East Falkland Island

Argentine soldiers invading East Falkland Island

Stanley from the air (Work of User: Tom L-C, CC BY SA 3.0, Wikimedia.org

**The town of Port Stanley (Work of CHK 46, CC BY SA 4.0
Wikimedia.org)**

**Princess Ann lays a wreath at the Falklands War Memorial
(Government House, Falkland Islands)**

The small village of Hill Cove on West Falkland Island

STRAITS OF MAGELLAN
PUNTA ARENAS

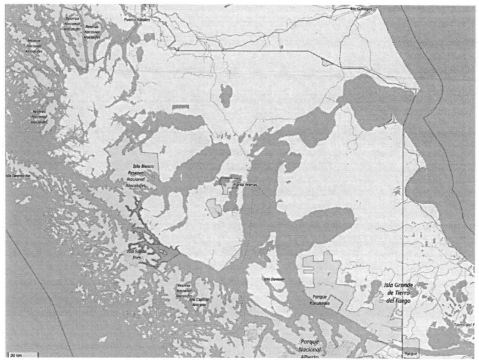

The Straits of Magellan and Tierra del Fuego (© OpenStreetMap contributors)

The Straits of Magellan connect the waters of the South Atlantic Ocean with those of the South Pacific Ocean, being a deep-water channel that is partly the result of movement along the plate boundary between the South American and Scotia Plates combined with glacial scour during the last ice age. The strait is about 515 kilometers or 320 miles in length and has many fjords that branch off of it. On its western margin, the numerous large offshore islands produce a landscape where multiple channels extend both north and south. The primary route cruise ships follow is northbound along the Smyth Channel. Depending upon the itinerary, the other commonly followed route is south around the western and southern margin of Tierra del Fuego utilizing the Beagle Channel. Freight traffic generally exits into the South Pacific, as negotiating the Smyth Channel adds days to any journey around the continent. Most large freighters and oil tankers use the straits simply because they are unable to transit the Panama Canal, thus their captains wish to get out to sea as rapidly as possible. Only cruise ships will negotiate the Smyth Channel because their transit north is based upon providing passengers with the breathtaking scenery of the fjord country.

The mountains that rise up north of the Straits of Magellan represent the southernmost Andes, showing both tectonic and volcanic forces. And the higher peaks have been extensively glaciated. Tierra del Fuego is a large piece of land, covering 48,101 square kilometers or 18,572 square miles. Technically the island is a part of the continent of South America, but separated by a combination of plate movement and glacial scour. There are hundreds of small islands on the Pacific side of Tierra del Fuego and northward along the coast of Chile. These are all geologically a part of the continent, but separated by glacially created channels. The landscape is akin to that of the Alaska-British Columbia coast, Norway and Greenland.

There are strong currents and several narrow spots, thus it is not possible for ship bridge crews to navigate the Straits of Magellan alone. There are also strong diurnal tides that must be understood so as to keep ships safe while they navigate through the straits. The Government of Chile provides pilots who will remain on board ship during the entire passage. Cruise ships that will be utilizing the Beagle Channel or Smyth Channel must provide accommodation and meals for the pilots since they may remain on board for up to ten days.

There are rich forests wherever the land is level enough and the winds are not overly strong for trees to have taken root. Forests or woodlands of southern beech and canelo, which is the southernmost coniferous tree on earth are found along the straits and on the island of Tierra del Fuego.

The landscape is spectacular to say the least. If the weather is clear, you will see mountains that can often be draped with fresh snow during summertime. The many islands and small fjords provide for a complex geography. Glimpses of major glacial fields higher up can be had during clear weather. But even when it is partly cloudy or stormy, the Straits of Magellan can be very dramatic. Entering from the Atlantic side is far less spectacular, as the land is initially part of the southern Patagonian plain. But when entering from the Pacific side, the Straits are a continuation of the already spectacular scenery seen coming south through the Smyth Channel or north up the Beagle Channel. Weather is a major factor in your ability to enjoy cruising through the straits and on to the southern margins of Tierra del Fuego via the Beagle Channel. The southern tip of South America is the most southerly landmass in these higher middle latitudes. If you look at a globe, you will see that there is no other land in the 50-degree latitude belt in the Southern Hemisphere. Thus the prevailing westerly winds roar around the planet, and when the approach these mountainous reaches of South America, the bring copious quantities of moisture plus gale force winds. Mariners from the 19th century called the 40-degree latitude belt the "Roaring 40's" and the 50-degree latitude belt the "Howling 50's. Finally beyond all land, approaching the Antarctic Continent, the 60-degree latitude belt was called the "Screaming 60's." Winds can blow through the Straits of Magellan at 144 to 160 kilometers or 90 to 100 miles per hour on a bright sunny day without there being any evidence of a storm.

HISTORY: During his 1520 circumnavigation of the globe, Ferdinand Magellan became the first European to navigate the straits that ultimately bear his name. The Spanish attempted to establish colonies on the northern shore in 1584, but by 1587 they were abandoned because of the fierce cold and inability to raise crops.

The British explorer Sir Francis Drake explored and mapped the straits, followed by other British military officers between the late 1500's and mid 1800's. Fear of British or French domination prompted Chile to declare the waters as their territory in 1843, but Argentina also wished to lay claim to the eastern portion of the straits. By 1848, Punta Arenas had been established. And by 1881, Argentina had relinquished any claim to the straits.

Until the opening of the Panama Canal in 1914, the straits were the main route of travel between the Atlantic and Pacific, especially for American shipping. But by the 1980's with the construction of super tankers and cargo vessels, the Panama Canal had become too small. Even with the building of new, larger locks today, there will still be many thousands of vessels plying the oceans that will need to use the Straits of Magellan because of their size. Thus the importance of this waterway will remain.

PUNTA ARENAS: This is the largest city in the world at the far southern latitude of 53 degrees. Punta Arenas has a population of just over 130,000 people. It is an important refueling and resupply port for large cargo vessels traveling around the continent because of their inability to transit the Panama Canal. The port also serves as a supply

station for many research vessels that are traveling to and from Antarctica.

The city is located on the northern shore of the Straits of Magellan on what is called the Brunswick Peninsula, a mountainous bulge in the southernmost of the continental Andes Mountains. It is located on a rather relatively flat grassy plain, but immediately backed up by thickly wooded slopes of the southern Andes.

Punta Arenas owes its earliest existence in 1843 to the establishment of a penal colony, but also with the settlement of free colonists. Twice there was violence when prisoners conducted a mutiny, first in 1851 and the second time in 1877 when they damaged a large part of the community. By the end of the 19th century, the discovery of gold and the establishment of sheep ranches began to show prosperity since Punta Arenas was the major supply, banking and medical center for the vast region along the straits.

Today Punta Arenas is the center of the Chilean oil exploration and development sector along with continued ranching, limited sustained yield forestry, fishing and its port services. And now it has become a major stop for cruise ships that are doing the Cone of South America during the Southern Hemisphere summer season. With many seal and penguin colonies, flights or cruises to Antarctica and tours inland to Torres del Paine National Park, Punta Arenas has become a very major tourist destination. Its airport has connecting flights via Santiago to many world destinations.

When you visit during summer, do not expect warm weather. From December to March it will most often be sunny, but daytime temperatures may only be in the upper 50's to low 60's. The average high temperature for the entire year is only 48.9 degrees Fahrenheit. And Punta Arenas is known for its very strong winds that blow through the straits. Wind speeds 160 kilometers or 100 miles per hour are not uncommon, and they can create a wind chill factor that is quite dramatic. Since 1986 when it was discovered that there was a major hole in the southern ozone layer, Punta Arenas has been the largest city to experience exposure to higher rates of damaging ultra violet radiation. For people who live there, the need to wear protective sunscreen is critical. Fortunately with the worldwide ban of CFC's, the ozone layer is starting to repair itself, but it will still take decades. Visitors who are only spending the day off a cruise ship need not be overly concerned about the UV exposure.

Most visitors coming off a cruise ship generally take one of the city tours or an all day tour out to see marine life along the shores. Few people attempt to venture off on their own, yet there are numerous taxis at the port with drivers who speak some English, but who are most accommodating and willing to show you the city and its surroundings. If you happen to be one of those who is adventurous and wishes to go off on your own, here are the major sights not to be missed in Punta Arenas, but excluding the nature reserves and scenic sights outside of the city, as those are best seen on one of your ship's tours:

* Plaza Munoz Gamero - The city's main plaza where on occasion local crafts people set up stalls to sell their wares

* Ferdinand Magellan Monument - Located in the center of the downtown, this is the most important monument in the city.

* Museo Regional de Magallanes - A popular museum representing the geography, anthropology and history of the entire region, but it can often be crowded when a ship is in port. The museum is open from 10:30 AM to 5 PM daily except Tuesday when it is closed.

* Catedral Sagrado Corazon - The beautiful Catholic cathedral for Punta Arenas. The cathedral is open daily, but no hours are posted.

* Salesian Museum - Another museum dedicated to the history of the Straits of Magellan, but not as well appreciated as the regional museum. The museum is open from 10 AM to 12:30 PM and again from 2 to 6 PM Tuesday thru Saturday, closed Sunday and Monday.

* Palacio Sara Braun - Located in the city center, this 19th century elegant mansion depicts how the wealthy of Punta Arenas lived during the city's economic boom. It is a worthwhile stop. It is open daily from 10:30 AM to 5 Pm except Tuesday when it is closed.

* Museo Naval y Maritimo - This small, but unique museum dedicated to the naval and maritime history of Punta Arenas is located at Pedro Montt 981 right in the city center. It is open 9:30 AM to 12:30 PM and from 2 to 6 PM Tuesday thru Saturday, closed Sunday and Monday.

* Monumento al Ovejero - Located in the residential area north of the city center along Avenida Bulnes, this collection of statues depicts and pays homage to the early pioneers of Punta Arenas. It is not a long walk if the weather is calm. Otherwise take a taxi to visit and also possibly tour other sites in the area.

* Fort Bulnes - Shows the way in which the early settlers endured the harsh environment. It is located about an hour outside of the city, but is of significance to those who are strongly interested in local history. You will need a private car or taxi to visit. Check on opening and closing hours before going, as none are posted on the web.

* Museo del Recuerdo - This is an open air museum that consists of a collection of pioneer buildings representing life in Punta Arenas during the 19th century. For those who are real history enthusiasts this is an interesting venue, but for others it is not. It does require a taxi ride because it is on the outskirts of the city, but you can combine visiting here with the Monumento al Ovejero. Open from 8:30 to 11:30 AM and from 2:30 to 6:30 PM Monday thru Friday and only 8:30 to 12"30 Saturday, closed Sunday.

* Nao Victoria Museo - Located about five miles north of the city center, you must take a taxi to reach this unique maritime museum. What it consists of are replicas of some of the most famous ships from the days of exploration. You will see Darwin's Beagle, the Shackleton lifeboat and the ship Magellan used when he discovered this famous strait. It is open from 8:30 AM to 7 PM daily.

The day spent in Punta Arenas can be quite enjoyable if you either take one of the extensive tours or hire a local taxi to guide you around the city. If you simply walk through the downtown area, you will be able to access many major highlights, but you will miss the full flavor of this still frontier city, largest urban center in these far southern latitudes.

Many ship passengers forgo a visit to Punta Arenas as a city and opt to visit one of the natural sites outside of the city, accomplishing this by joining one of the organized tours. I recommend this rather than attempting to go on your own with a taxi or having the ship provide a car and driver/guide. The most common wildlife you will see are penguins, but you will also be able to enjoy the scenery along the straits. If you wish to see some of the scenery, but are not that fascinated with penguins, you can have one of the local taxi drivers take you outside of the city to the higher elevations above Punta Arenas where you can see some of the Magellanic Forest landscape along with sweeping views out over the straits.

One unique place to visit not far from the city is El Galpon, a shed where sheep shearing demonstrations are presented along with a variety of exhibits regarding the rural life of the sheep rancher. You can combine a visit here with the scenic drive noted above. They also have a restaurant serving traditional Chileno meals typical of ranch life. They aim their activities toward cruise visitors and are always open during days when ships are in port, but do not publish specific hours.

DINING OUT: If you are traveling south from Buenos Aires, this will be your first chance to try Chileno cuisine. If you are traveling to Buenos Aires, and if you have enjoyed some of the true Chileno dishes, this will be your last chance. Given the cold weather, a nice hot meal will be a nice way to warm up to continue your sightseeing. Such dishes as pastel de chocolo, empanadas or grilled/fried conger eel are so much a part of the traditional cuisine. Here are my luncheon recommendations:

* Kiosco Roca - In the heart of the city at Roca 875, this small restaurant has become famous for its sandwiches, picada, banana and milkshakes and other luncheon dishes. Open from 7 AM to 7 PM Monday thru Friday and 8 AM to 1 PM Saturday, closed Sunday.

* Amaranta Teahouse - In the city center at Avenida Colon 822-B, this small teahouse serves salads, pasta and outstanding desserts. It is the type of place you can come for a light lunch or simply for tea and dessert. Open 10 AM to 9 PM Monday thru Saturday and 4 to 9 PM on Sunday.

* La Marmita - This is the place for fresh seafood, located at Plaza Sampaio 678 just north of the city center. Their menu features fresh seafood, vegetarian dishes and also a selection of meat entrees. Everything is well prepared and nicely presented. Open 12:30 to 3 PM and 1 to 11 PM Monday thru Friday, with extended time to Midnight Friday. Saturday hours are Midnight to Noon, 12:30 to 3:30 PM and 7 PM to Midnight.

* Cafe Imigrante - Located in the city center at Quillota 599. They are primarily a dinner oriented restaurant but starting with late lunches of sandwiches, pastries and fresh juices.. Open from 2:30 to 9 PM daily, closed on Sunday.

There are many more cafes and restaurants along with numerous dessert shops. Remember that many immigrants from Germany, Austria and Eastern Europe chose to settle in Southern Chile because they liked the cold environment that reminded them of home. Thus there is a strong emphasis upon fantastic desserts.

SHOPPING: One would not expect Punta Arenas to have much shopping of interest, but this is where you would be wrong. I will point out some of the unique shopping opportunities below:

* Zona Franca - Located on the north side of the city is the special Zona Franca, a duty free shopping zone that contains a variety of shops selling everything from fine European chocolates to designer clothes to outdoor sporting goods. There are fine perfumes, watches and jewelry. And there are shops specializing in electronics. How much cheaper you

will find the zone is dependent upon where you are from. Prices definitely are less than you would find in Buenos Aires or Santiago. The shops are only open on weekdays, so if your cruise lands on Saturday or Sunday, you are out of luck. You will need to take a taxi because the zone is way to far for walking.

* Espacio Urbano Pionero Mall - Touted as the southernmost shopping mall in the world, rightly so it is. It contains three major Chilean department stores, including Ripley, Falabella and La Polar. It also contains numerous shops, a supermarket and a food court. Once again, you will need to go by taxi, as it is too far to walk from where ships dock. The mall is open daily from 10 AM to 9 PM.

* Shops around the main plaza sell a variety of locally made craft items, and on warmer days some locals set up small stalls inside the main plaza itself.

The city of Punta Arenas (© OpenStreetMap contributors)

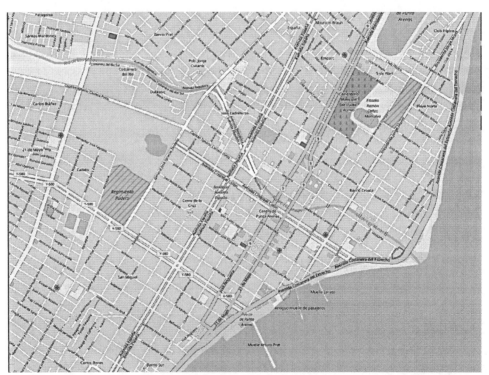

The city center of Punta Arenas (© OpenStreetMap contributors)

The Magellanic Forest west of Punta Arenas

Typical mountain landscape west of Punta Arenas

179

Looking over the city center of Punta Arenas

Looking north over residential Punta Arenas

In the downtown center of Punta Arenas

A mix of old and new buildings alongside the main plaza of Punta Arenas

Ferdinand Magellan looks out over Plaza de Armas, heart of Punta Arenas

Wealthy residential suburb of Punta Arenas

The outdoor Pioneer's Museum in Punta Arenas

Magellanic Penguins are the city's neighbors

TIERRA DEL FUEGO /USHUAIA

Across the Straits of Magellan is the large island of Tierra del Fuego. This mountainous island and its companion smaller islands are the southernmost major pieces of real estate in the Western Hemisphere. The steep mountains are deeply indented by deep-water fjords, scoured by glacial ice. The main island, which extends for nearly 200 miles on its north-south axis and nearly 300 miles on its east-west axis, having 48,101 square kilometers or 18,572 square miles, is divided between Argentina and Chile. The major portion of the island, 61.4 percent belongs to Chile, while Argentina has the eastern part of the island, occupying 34.5 percent of the land area. Through military and political pressure during the 19th century, Chile controls the entire Strait of Magellan.

It was once inhabited by very primitive tribes of natives who hunted, fished and gathered in the most basic of fashions. Lights from their campfires were seen by the first explorers who referred to the island as the land of fires, thus Tierra del Fuego. The Yaghan tribe is believed to have arrived some 10,000 years ago, were the major tribal group and essentially a primitive stone age people. The Yaghan and Selk'nam people were brought under Christian teaching, but ultimately disease took the majority. Only a handful of natives still live today, but they are found in the towns or on the mainland, no longer living by their primitive means.

There was very little initial interest in settlement on Tierra del Fuego until 1879 when placer gold was discovered on the Chilean side. The island had been claimed by both nations, but in 1881, a boundary treaty was signed after the establishment of the few towns on both sides of the island, today serving as the major settlements.

To reach the Argentine side of the island by road necessitates crossing first into Chile, then ferrying across and re crossing back into Argentina. Settlement is rather limited on both sides of the border as a result of the harsh cold, rainy and windy climate of Tierra del Fuego. The province within Argentina of the same name has less than 135,000 total residents. There is little productive land on Tierra del Fuego, but some gold is still mined, and limited grazing potential combined with fishing provides for the few inhabitants of the Argentine section of the island. Crossing to the Chilean side is also done by ferryboat out of

Punta Arenas. There are no major communities on the Chilean side of the island and the population is less than 20,000.

The major economic activities that support the island's meager population are oil and gas production on the Atlantic shore and at the eastern end of the Straits of Magellan, the raising of sheep on large estancias and tourism, especially in the area of ecotourism. Rio Grande is the slightly larger city and provincial capital, having just over 67,000 residents. It is also home to two small electronics assembly plants. But it is not a tourist destination because it is located on the eastern coast and all of the more rugged mountainous scenery is found along the Beagle Channel on the south and west coast.

THE BEAGLE CHANNEL: This important channel separates the main island of Tierra del Fuego from the smaller islands along its southern and western coastline, both in Argentina and Chile. It is a deep water channel, having been carved by glacial scour. The channel is around 242 kilometers or 150 miles long and averages three miles in width. Thus major shipping uses the Drake Passage, the stormy waters to the south that separate South America from Antarctica, or the Straits of Magellan. Use of the Beagle Channel necessitates having a local pilot on board, one who knows the intricate details of the waterway, its currents and tides. Cruise ships use the channel because of its intense scenic qualities, traversing between Punta Arenas and Ushuaia on a regular basis during the summer months. Some ships will venture outside of the channel to navigate past Cape Horn, the tiny island that marks the southernmost piece of land in the Western Hemisphere. But weather plays the major role and often precludes such a passage.

The channel takes its name from the HMS Beagle, the ship that transported Charles Darwin on two voyages where he was the scientist who studied the flora and fauna of the entire region, including the Atacama Desert and Galapagos Islands to the north. These two voyages were instrumental in Darwin formulating his theories on the progression of life through adaptation to the environment by the means of evolution. His most famous work, *On the Origin of Species,* touched off a firestorm regarding the meaning of evolution, a controversy that still rages in the minds of some pseudo-scientists and many lay people.

The waters of the Beagle Channel have been the site of several naval incidents between Argentina and Chile over ownership of the many islands. It was not until the signing of the Treaty of Peace and Friendship in 1984 that the two countries agreed to a final settlement. As a result, Chile received the majority of the islands.

USHUAIA: Most of the Argentine province's population lives in the coastal capital of Rio Grande or in Ushuaia, which is located on the Beagle Channel. The residents claim it to be the southernmost city in the world, a large sign proclaiming "Al Fin del Mundo," meaning the bottom or end of the world. But is Ushuaia the southernmost city in the world? Argentina claims it to be so, but Chile claims Puerto Williams, located across the Beagle Channel, but having only 2,000 residents, is the most southerly city on earth. Ushuaia has 56,956 residents. So it all depends upon point of view as to what constitutes a city.

Ushuaia owes its founding to British missionaries and to the first visit of the HMS Beagle in 1833, but no permanent structures were built until 1870. Later in 1873, the president of Argentina proposed using the small camp as a penal colony patterned after Port Arthur in Tasmania. It was not until after the settling of the border with Chile in 1881 that work began to develop a prison, which was completed in 1896. This remote location was subjected to not only isolation, but several epidemics such as typhus and measles decimated the early outpost. The prison remained viable until 1947, and then the Argentine navy took over the facility, but it eventually became the maritime museum.

Ushuaia has become a popular destination for tourists. Its attraction is not only its most southerly location, but also the island possesses a haunting beauty and serenity, and it offers outdoor adventures, which include hiking, mountain biking and deep-sea sport fishing. The small port services cruise ships, military vessels and research traffic destined for the Antarctic Continent. The airfield at Ushuaia is also the closest to bases located in the Western Hemisphere sector of the Antarctic. And Ushuaia is the jumping off point to a small offshore island, across the border in Chile, that is the single southernmost piece of land in the Western Hemisphere, once notorious among mariners because of the fierce storms that whip across its waters during much of the year. The island is of course Cape Horn, and it can only be visited on a few days each summer, as even then the winds are too strong for most boats to access it. Because of its importance, the government of Chile has made it a national park. Some cruise itineraries include rounding Cape Horn, but like going to the Falkland Islands, it is subject to weather conditions. With the strong westerly winds roaring around the globe totally unobstructed by land, they pick up great force. Tierra del Fuego and the southern portions of Patagonia are the only landmasses to intercept these winds. Thus at Cape Horn on a bright sunny day, it is not impossible for ocean swells to be 9 to 16 meters or 30 to 50 feet, far greater than any cruise ship captain is willing to submit has ship and passengers to experiencing. It is far too dangerous.

The city of Ushuaia resembles communities found in Alaska, not only with regard to the surroundings, but also the ramshackle wood architecture. The settlement of the island mirrors that of Alaska with gold, fishing and seal hunting having brought primarily northern Europeans to this isolated region. There is virtually no semblance of traditional Spanish Argentina to be found in Ushuaia. Both the architecture and the people themselves reflect more of Germanic and Scandinavian influence, giving Ushuaia the same type of flavor as that seen in Bariloche and the Chilean Lake District.

As was true in Punta Arenas, most cruise ship visitors to Ushuaia spend the day on one of the tours into the countryside to enjoy the scenery or wildlife. The major site is Tierra del Fuego National Park just west of the city and extending to the border of Chile. Visits include stops at many scenic vistas or riding the special narrow gauge train into the interior for a short distance. Some tour itineraries for the day will include nature walks along the trails available for visitors. This gives those who seek more solitude and a chance to view wildlife with fewer disturbances the opportunity not found on the larger bus tours.

For those seeking natural beauty and/or a chance to view fauna on their own it is possible to either arrange through your ship's shore office a private car and driver/guide or you may hire a local taxi driver, as most know the surrounding areas outside of town. And most do speak some English. Places to visit outside of Ushuaia include:
* Laguna Esmeralda - A magnificent glacial lake with a dramatic mountain backdrop, but this visit entails a two-hour hike from where the car is left.
* Bahia Lapatia - Within Tierra del Fuego National Park, but more secluded and not on the general tourist agenda.
* Cerro Castor - Just north of this city, this high mountain is the local ski and snowboarding venue. During summer a storm can dump fresh snow on the mountain slopes at any time, so if you happen to be there at the right time, you can ski or snowboard.
* Lago Roca - Another quiet and very scenic remote location for those with the adventurous spirit.

* Estancia Haberton - Outside of Ushuaia along the coast 85 kilometers east of Ushuaia, this estancia gives you a chance to explore one of the principal economic activities steeped in the history of settlement. You will need a car and driver or local taxi for the one-hour drive. It is open for visits by cruise passengers, but does not post specific hours.

* A short drive along the coast road into Tierra del Fuego National Park to the terminus of the scenic railroad. This enables those who do not want to spend much time away from town a chance to at least see some of the beautiful countryside.

Within the small city of Ushuaia there are a few things to occupy your time if you choose to only walk around the city center or venture by taxi to a few of the cultural highlights. They include:

* Museo Historico - Located in the former governor's palace on Calle Maipú #465, this is an excellent museum providing exhibits on Tierra del Fuego history. It is open daily from 9 AM to 8 PM.

* Museo del Fin del Mundo - A small museum with local artifacts, and also traces the early penal history of Ushuaia. The museum is a bit hard to find, located on the east end of town at Calle Maipú #173. Open Monday thru Saturday from 10 AM to 5 PM, closed Sunday.

* Galeria Tematica - A museum devoted to the early people of Tierra del Fuego and the visit of Charles Darwin. Open Noon to 6 PM Tuesday thru Saturday, closed Sunday.

* Museo Maritimo y del Presidio de Ushuaia - Housed in the former prison barracks, this museum traces the maritime history of the region. It is located at Avenida San Martin #152 and is open from 10 AM to 8 PM daily except Sunday.

* Iglesia de la Merced - A beautiful and tranquil Catholic church. No hours are posted, but the church is generally open during the day.

* Plaza Malvinas - This is a memorial to the losses Argentina suffered during the 1982 war with the British over the Falkland Islands.

DINING OUT: As with all the smaller ports, the ship will be leaving in the early to mid evening, so dining out will be confined to lunch. You will find that among those restaurants open at lunch, there will be a strong emphasis upon Italian, French and German cuisine, reflecting the immigrants who came to Ushuaia. I recommend the following:

* Kalma Resto - This is one of the most acclaimed restaurants in Ushuaia. It is located at Calle Antarida Argentina 57 in the city center and is closed on Sunday.. The menu is essentially Argentino, and you will find many traditional dishes, including a variety of roasted meats. And their desserts do justice to the European influences on the city. Prices are a bit high for Ushuaia, but well worthwhile. If you ship is

staying into the evening, this is a great dinner spot, open from 7 to 11 PM.

* Kaupe - This is another highly acclaimed restaurant, located just a few blocks north of Avenida San Martin at Avenida Roca 470. It is also closed on Sunday, but open daily for dinner from 6:30 to 11 PM. There is a strong emphasis upon fresh seafood and the style of cooking is a fusion of Argentino and French.

* Paseo Garibaldi - Located at Gobernador Deloqui #133, this restaurant and pub is perfect for visitors who are seeking the true flavors of Argentina. Their diverse menu is superb. Open from 12:30 to 2:30 PM Tuesday thru Saturday and 7 to 11:30 PM Tuesday thru Sunday.

* Ramos Generales - This is a fine restaurant for lunch, located in the city center at Avenida Maipu 749. It features great soups, lamb dishes, sandwiches and pastas. They are open daily from 9 AM to Midnight and possibly your best bet for lunch.

SHOPPING: There is very little shopping in Ushuaia apart from a few stores that sell the usual tourist kitsch. If you are interested in buying leather goods or clothing and did not do so in Buenos Aires or Santiago, there are a couple of small clothing shops for men and women on Avenida San Martin in the heart of Ushuaia. I do recommend:

* Paseo de los Artisanos Enriqueta Gastelumendi located at Plaza 25 de Mayo that features a collection of stalls selling handcraft items from Patagonia. The selection is moderate, but all the items are handmade. Some of the artisanos will be at their stalls actually working on a piece when you visit.

* Paseo del Fuego is the main shopping mall for Ushuaia, located about two miles east of the city center. You will need to take a taxi to get there. It is located on Avenida Perito Moreno 1460. The mall is open from 10 AM to 10 PM and offers stores similar to those found in the city center, but at least under one roof, especially if the weather should not be good.

*Honeker el Chocolate de Ushuaia located on Avenida San Martin 880 produces some dynamic chocolate that is excellent. They are open from 10 AM to 10 PM daily.

FINAL WORDS: Along the Beagle Channel extending westward and north from Ushuaia there are many deep fjords with active glaciers at their head. These fjords are still in the process of being carved by tongues of ice from the South Patagonia Ice field, one of the largest outside of the Antarctic or Greenland. Depending upon the size of ship you are on, if it is small in size and weight, being less than 20,000 tons, you may be able to experience sailing up one of these fjords to visit a remote glacier. From personal experience I do know that on Silversea's smaller ships if the journey around Cape Horn is cancelled due to weather, and if the Chileno pilots are willing, the transit up a narrow fjord to visit Glacier Garibaldi may be in the offing. It is a most spectacular experience. Smaller vessels in the explorer category do visit glaciers along this stretch of the Beagle Channel, an event to be savored. But any of the large cruise ships are unable to navigate these fjords or be able to turn around for the outbound journey. But you will still enjoy the magnificence of the scenery while transiting the Beagle Channel

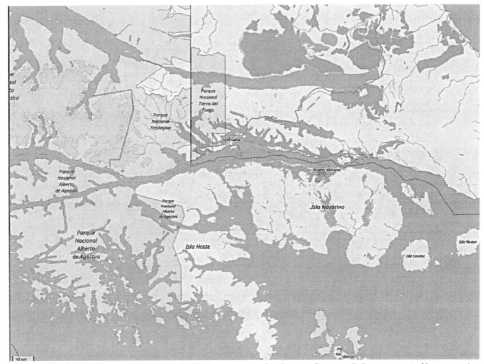

A map showing the Beagle Channel (© OpenStreetMap contributors)

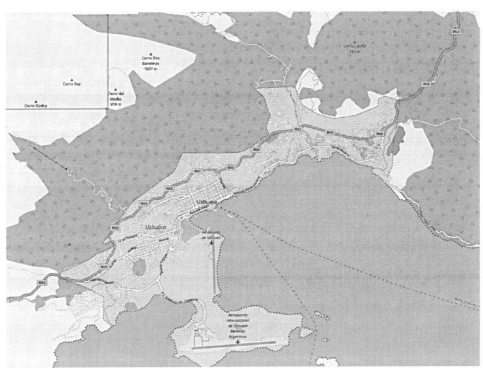

The city of Ushuaia (© OpenStreetMap contributors)

The ethereal beauty of the Beagle Channel

A portion of the great ice field on Tierra del Fuego

The remote and spectacular Garibaldi Glacier on Tierra del Fuego

The remote fjords around the edges of Tierra del Fuego are seldom explored

In the snow covered mountains above Ushuaia

A mid summer scene above Ushuaia, not too unusual

Fresh water streams flow down from the high Tierra del Fuego peaks

Ushuaia after a mid summer snowfall

Avenida San Martin in downtown Ushuaia

A typical residential street in Ushuaia

One of numerous penguin colonies outside of Ushuaia

FJORDS OF CHILE

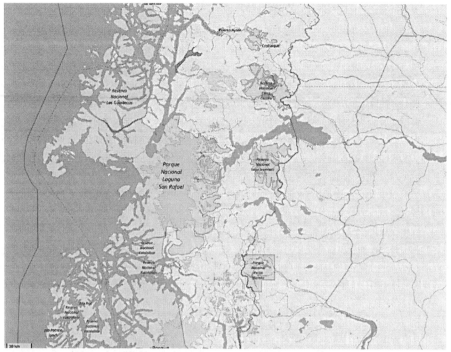

The northern region of fjords (© OpenStreetMap contributors)

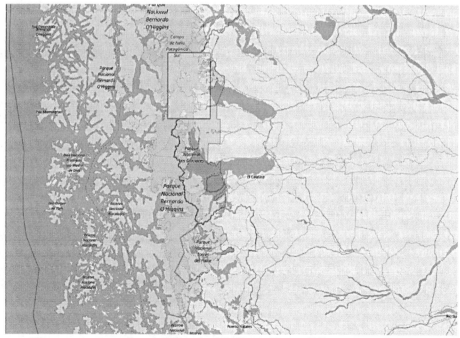

The central region of fjords (© OpenStreetMap contributors)

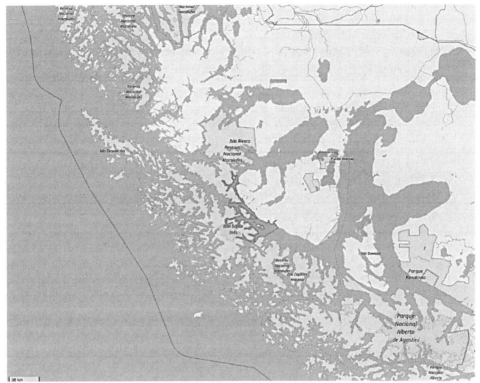
The southern region of fjords (© OpenStreetMap contributors)

The southern third of Chile's long coastline, starting at Puerto Montt and extending all the way to Cape Horn, is a land of deep oceanic fjords, protecting offshore islands and high mountain ice fields. This is the second most remote and forbidding fjord coastline after Greenland, much longer than the coastline of southern Alaska and British Columbia, but comparable in length to Norway. The fjords are not as long with regard to how deep into the mountains they penetrate when contrasted to Norway, but they are every bit as magnificent. The number of offshore islands and the intricate network of channels separating them from the mainland is far more extensive than any of the other fjord coasts already noted. And only the coast of Greenland is more sparsely populated.

The fjord coast might be the least known or visited part of Chile, but even in this nation of incredible scenery, this region is the ultimate in natural spectacle. The first European to ever see the mountains and fjords of southern Chile was Ferdinand Magellan, who in 1520 sailed through the straits that now bear his name. Until the Panamas Canal opened in 1914, the Straits of Magellan were the vital link between the Atlantic and Pacific Oceans. Today these waters still serve the large

199

tankers, freighters and even aircraft carriers that on occasion need to transit between the two great oceans. In 2004, the aircraft carrier U. S. S. Ronald Reagan traversed the straits en route from Norfolk, Virginia to its new home in San Diego.

The inside passage does not run continuously between the Straits of Magellan and Puerto Montt. There is one massive mountain spur that extends westward to the Pacific, and this necessitates a detour out into the open South Pacific for only a few hours. Coming northbound this detour is prior to visiting Laguna San Rafael and southbound it follows after the glacial visit. A series of maps at the end of this chapter shows you the nature of the fjords in this region.

THE ENGLISH NARROWS: When cruising through the inside passage, what normally amazes passengers is the total absence of human presence. It takes approximately two days between the Straits of Magellan and Laguna San Rafael, and during that passage the ship will only pass one very tiny village that can easily be missed. The highlight of human presence is a small statue of the Madonna at a place called English Narrows where the inside passage is exceptionally tight for medium size vessels. The channel is only 182 meters or 200 yards wide and 11 miles in length. If the ship is about to face strong winds, then normally passage is delayed, as it makes the passage too dangerous. But surprisingly the channel is one of the deepest of the fjords of Chile, measuring more than 1067 meters or 3,500 feet to the bottom. Mariners have developed a custom of throwing coins to the Madonna and offering prayers for safe passage.

LAGUNA SAN RAFAEL: One of the highlights of the more in depth cruise itineraries is a visit to Laguna San Rafael and the San Rafael Glacier. After a brief detour out to sea if coming northbound, the ship re enters the northern inside passage and proceeds south to the southern margin of the Moraleda Channel. Here the ship will drop anchor because it is too risky for a major ship to proceed closer to the glacier and the thousands of icebergs that are created during the warmer months of summer. Guests will be transferred to small craft for the journey into Laguna San Rafael, which is a fresh water lake formed as the glacier has retreated. Guests will wear life vests because occasional calving of the glacier can produce a miniature tsunami and the tour operator takes no chances. This is an exciting visit, as the small craft will take close to the massive San Rafael Glacier, one of several outlets for the Northern Patagonia Ice Field, which straddles the border between Argentina and Chile. This is the most northerly ice field in South America covering 4,145 square kilometers or 1,600 square miles. However, due to climate change the ice field is slowly shrinking, but its elevation and the continued winter chill guarantee that it will be here for centuries, just not as large as it was a century past.

Visiting the face of the San Rafael Glacier is a dramatic experience. As the vessel sails into Laguna San Rafael, small chunks of ice are slowly replaced by larger pieces that can be classed as icebergs. And if the weather is slightly warmer than normal, you will see large pieces of the glacial face plunge into the water. This is what geologists call calving. It is very spectacular and exciting to see. Initially you hear a cracking sound if the piece is quite large. Then it slowly begins to break away and suddenly it plunges to the water below. The wave that rolls outward follows the same laws of physics that would be seen when the seafloor heaves during a catastrophic earthquake, generating a tsunami. The boat will only get as close to the glacial face as conditions permit on the day you visit. The company operating the tour will always try to bring the vessel as close to the glacial face as is safely possible.

AISÉN FJORD: Either following the visit to the San Rafael Glacier if you are traveling northbound, or the day prior on southbound cruises, the ship will sail into the beautiful Aisén Fjord, which extends 80 kilometers or 50 miles into the mountains in the same way that Norwegian fjords do. The cruise up Aisén Fjord is one of the most magnificent portions of the entire journey. Starting at dawn, your ship will slowly make its way deep into this fjord, having left the main north south channel. Aisén Fjord is so reminiscent of Norway with its steep walls rising to snow covered heights, and its lower reaches covered in thick forest. All that is missing are the mountain farms that cling to the upper slopes in Norway. Aisén Fjord throughout most of its length is totally unspoiled. Only at its eastern end is where you will find any significant development with the towns of Puerto Chacabuco and Puerto Aisén.

At one time Puerto Aisén was the major port for fishing or commercial vessels. The eruption of Mount Hudson in 1991 necessitated the building of a new port nine miles farther down the fjord. Chacabuco itself is a relatively new small port town that replaced the nearby town of Puerto Aisén. It was the original regional port, located at the mouth of the Aisén River, which became choked in ash from a 1991 volcanic eruption of nearby Mount Hudson.

Your destination is this new dock at Puerto Chacabuco where several activities await. For those who wish to remain close to the ship, there are nature walks along the fjord and into the forests. On some cruise itineraries there are tours by boat or bus along the upper end of the fjord. And the longest tour is inland to the regional capital city of Coihaique, which sits at the base of the Andean crest. If your cruise line operates a shuttle into Puerto Aisén, you will find a rather quiet local trade center that offers little or nothing for the visitor. I cannot even offer any suggestions with regard to shopping or dining.

COIHAIQUE: Settlement in southern Chile began in the early 19th century when forts were established at Bulnes and Punta Arenas, opening up a few of the less rugged areas for sheep ranching and timber cutting. Even today, there are very few towns or settlements south of Puerto Montt, most being coastal fishing villages. As noted previously, roads into this region are few and for the most part unimproved. The country is just too rugged for adequate building of roads, similar in nature to the panhandle region of Alaska where roads are also for the most part absent. It is possible to drive south from Puerto Montt with one ferry connection across the Golfo Corcovado as far as Coihaique, a distance of almost 480 kilometers or 300 miles via rather narrow road. Coihaique is tucked into the side of the Andes, just inland from the coast in a beautiful, but somewhat windswept valley where limited ranching has been developed. It is a remote, yet intensely breathtaking region of high peaks, grassy slopes, groves of forest and fast flowing rivers. Despite its isolation, it has become an important getaway for those seeking the out of doors away from civilization. Yet the town of Coihaique possesses the major conveniences of any small service town in central Chile. With a population of 37,000, it serves as the administrative capital of this vast and lonely region.

Your drive to Coihaique will take about 90 minutes from Puerto Chacabuco, but this will be one of the most scenic and breathtaking trips you have taken. And there are numerous photo stops en route giving you ample opportunity to enjoy the scenery. There is little to do in Coihaique other than walking around this remote regional capital and visiting the local museum. It is the drive there and back that makes the outing a success. The region is so isolated and has so few facilities that obtaining a private car and driver/guide or hiring a local taxi in Puerto Chacabuco is essentially out of the question. Thus if you wish to make this journey, it must be on one of the organized tours offered by your cruise line. I generally do not personally choose to go on group tours, but I must admit that I did thoroughly enjoy the one Silversea offered to Coihaique.

The tour to Coihaique generally lasts for anywhere from four to six hours. Some cruise lines will provide a buffet lunch at one of the nice roadhouses en route while others will not. Since you cannot undertake this journey on your own, you will not have a choice of restaurants nor will you have any chance to shop. Thus I am not providing a list of venues for dining or shopping in Coihaique.

The road continues on from Coihaique across a pass in the Andes and into the Patagonia region of Argentina where it connects with the main coastal highway on the Atlantic side of the country. From the junction with the main highway it is then possible to drive south back across the border and on to Punta Arenas, the most southerly major city on the continent. Within Chile, however, there are no roads leading south along the coast to Puerto Natales or Punta Arenas, a distance of over 600 miles. You must first cross into Argentina and then back across the border to Puerto Natales or Punta Arenas. This is the emptiest part of the nation, even more remote than the Atacama Desert in the far north.

Puerto Natales, located far from the open ocean along a deep-water fjord is the service town for the most spectacular of all of Chile's national parks. Torres del Paine, a World Biosphere Reserve since 1978, is comprise of glacially sculpted towers and horns, carved out of sheer granite, rising up above the fjord and surrounding forest to heights of nearly 3,050 meters or 10,000 feet. This is a locale of unparalleled scenic quality, but it is also a region of capricious weather. Fierce winds, blustery rain storms and snow at higher elevations make winter a season to be avoided, but even during the somewhat mild summer, unpredictable weather can change the calm beauty to one of tumult in minutes. The park exhibits varied types of southern Andean vegetation depending upon slope and exposure. There are lush forests, wind blown pampas and scrubby woodlands, but all are inhabited by a diverse wildlife which includes guanaco, vicuña, fox, puma, condors, flamingos and varied fresh and salt water fish.

Torres del Paine has become a major destination for visitors, resulting in the development of several first class lodges within the park as well as varied accommodation in Puerto Natales. This is one destination that many foreign visitors to Chile consider a must on their itinerary despite its great isolation from the heart of the country. It is possible to fly from Santiago into Puerto Natales, which is then only a short distance from the park. There is also a road connection to Punta Arenas, a distance of just over 193 kilometers or 120 miles. It is also possible to travel by long distance ferry from Puerto Natales to Puerto Montt, but this journey takes one week, and is essentially a cruise through the fjord country but without all of the frills of a commercial cruise ship. Thus if passengers on board a cruise ship traveling between Buenos Aires and Valparaiso wish to visit Torres del Paine, it must be a pre or post cruise visit by air from Santiago. And I recommend it highly for those who have both the time and adventurous spirit. I guarantee that it would be one of the most incredible journeys you will have ever undertaken.

The Madonna of English Narrows

The face of the San Rafael Glacier

Everyone wears a life preserver when getting close to the San Rafael Glacier

The numerous icebergs spawned by the San Rafael Glacier

Just after sunrise in Aisen Fjord

The peaceful beauty of Aisén Fjord

Following the Aisén River to Coihaique

Looking down on the town of Coihaique

Exhibits dedicated to early pioneers in Coihaique

In the center of Coihaique

A sumptuous afternoon repast at a Coihaique restaurant

Chileno buffet service is very appetizing

CHILE'S LAKE DISTRICT

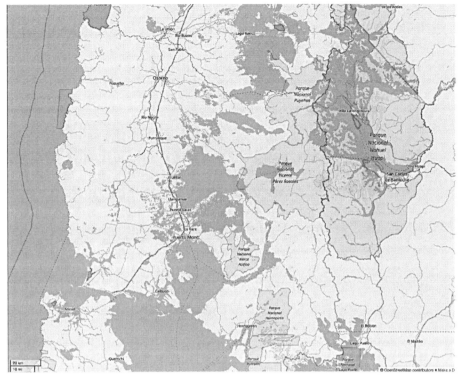

The Lake District of Chile (© OpenStreetMap contributors)

The Chilean Lake district is one of the world's most sought after locales with regard to its scenic qualities. It is the pride and joy of Chile, regarded by Chilenos as the number one tourist destination within the country. This is a land of glacial lakes that are deep blue and crystal clear, backed up by a chain of perfectly formed, snow-capped volcanic cones. To the west are the coastal hills and the South Pacific Ocean where the coastline is relatively smooth, but rugged. To the south, the Golfo Corcovado indents itself into the coast and this is the start of the fjord country that extends south for the next 1,450 kilometers or 900 miles to the tip of Tierra del Fuego. Fast flowing rivers rush from melting glaciers and snowfields to empty into the many glacially created lakes or off to the ocean less than 160 kilometers or 100 miles away, most writhing in white water as they crash over the rugged, rocky landscape.

The entire region is within a maritime climatic regime, one that has sufficient rainfall throughout the year, but in particular during the winter months. The forests are thick and in many locations they are classed as temperate rainforests. Stands of tall araucaria, coihue and cipres (early species of conifer) along with southern beech mirror the beauty found in British Columbia and Alaska, only with a totally different array of plant life. Most of the species found in the Lake District are not very tolerant of extreme cold, thus the timberline is relatively low, leaving the upper slopes of the mountains to stand bare and bold against the sky, allowing the winter snow to appear to be much whiter because it is seen on bare rock.

Much of the dramatic beauty of this region is owed to the end of the Pleistocene, or ice age, when the retreating glacial ice disarranged the drainage, damming some streams, gouging deep basins and providing a source of water to create the many lakes that comprise the heart of this region. It has become the focus of outdoor sports that include kayaking, white water rafting, sailing, trekking, hiking and camping. And in winter there is skiing, as this is one of Chile's prime winter sports venue. Or if one is not energetic, just sitting and taking in the panorama can also enable a person to feel the majestic quality of the region.

The Lake District was once home to the Mapuche Indians, fierce warriors who inhibited settlement of the country. Today there are few Mapuche left, but those who have survived have reservations within the Lake District, which is their traditional home. But the majority of the pioneers who settled here came from northern and eastern Europe. When immigrants began to come into Chile from other than Spain, many sought out country that was similar to their homeland. Only the Germans, Scandinavians and Slavic peoples of Eastern Europe felt at home amid the thick forests and under a chill climate. Thus the Chilean Lake District to this day is more Germanic and Slavic than it is Romanic. Spanish may still be the official language, but it is not the tongue spoken in thousands of homes across the region.

Settlement did destroy many forested areas, especially in the lowland valleys, as pioneers cut timber, plowed up the soil and built their towns. Today, the lowlands are agriculturally productive, raising delicate berries, fruits such as apples and pears, herding dairy cattle and processing the milk into a variety of products. The entire flavor of the area speaks to a northern European lifestyle, more reminiscent of the Pacific Northwest of the United States than what one would expect in a Latin American country. But other than the slightly drier eastern slopes of the Andes in Argentina, there is nowhere else in all of Latin America that possesses this type of natural environment. Many of the interior towns and farms are, however, located in the shadow of beautiful, but potentially dangerous volcanoes such as Osorno and Puyehue, but like in the American Pacific Northwest, the threat is generally in the back of people's minds. However, in April 2015, with little or no warning, Calbuco Volcano just east of Puerto Montt erupted with intense fury, sending an ash cloud up as high as 1,980 meters or 65,000 feet. Several small villages close to the mountain flank did suffer damage, but fortunately few people had chosen to settle on the mountain's lower flank. And the prevailing winds sent most of the ash eastward across the mountain crest into Argentina.

The larger towns were built along the coast where fishermen could take advantage of the sea's bounty and where timber and dairy products could be exported to the rest of the nation and to the outside world. In these larger towns, the European flavor is as predominant as in the rural hinterlands. Wood buildings, most often painted white and with steeply pitched roofs abound. Many species of deciduous trees, both native and European, have been planted, giving the autumn months that special color that is characteristic of high latitude lands.

The entire Lake District benefits today from tourism, especially during the summer. This is the playground of South America with its cool weather, crystal clear lakes and towering mountains. Add to this the Germanic and Slavic flavor, and it offers people from all over the continent a taste of Europe without the overseas trip. The only analogy to this would be when Americans and Canadians visit Canada's distinctly French province of Quebéc. Not only does the Lake District have great appeal to South Americans who can afford to make the trip, but it is also the most favored venue on the continent for foreign visitors, especially North Americans. The raw natural beauty can be enjoyed from within the comfort zone of elegant hotels and lodges, and accompanied by delicious food that offers a blend of Chileno and European tastes. Recognizing the value of this region, the government of Chile has set aside many portions of the mountain and lower elevation forests as national park land, thus not only preserving rare tree species, but ensuring that the region's great beauty is not marred by future expansion or development.

Although the Lake District is not highly urbanized, there are numerous medium size cities that have become focal centers of development both for tourism and the region's other activities such as food processing and the lumber industry. The three most important cities in the Lake District are Valdivia, Temuco and Puerto Montt.

Valdivia is the oldest city in the region, its original founding dating back to colonial times, being first colonized in 1552. The city is located at the confluence of two important rivers, the Rio Cruces and the Rio Calle-Calle. It is about 48 kilometers or 30 miles up the Rio Valdivia estuary from the open ocean. It was initially a defensive stronghold for the Spanish in their slow and ongoing war with the Mapuche Indians. By the 1850's, German immigrants began to arrive and settle in and around the town, bringing with them a new cultural flavor that would eventually come to dominate. Today the city's economy is based upon the raising of fine livestock in the surrounding hinterlands, the production of beer, the processing of wood and pulp products and of course tourism. The architectural flavor of Valdivia is one of the city's major factors with regard to its distinctness, giving one the impression of being in Germany rather than Chile. Today's population for the Valdivia region is around 100,000 people.

North of Valdivia, located in an interior valley along the Rio Imperial is the city of Temuco, the largest city of the Lake District. It has a metropolitan population of 270,000 people, giving it quite a cosmopolitan flavor and a significant skyline. It does not have the history of Valdivia, having only been founded in 1881 initially as a governmental center to administer to the remaining Mapuche Indians who were put on reservations in the surrounding region. Slowly it grew into a trade center as settlers of various nationalities, in particular Germanic and Slavic, moved into the rich river valley to farm and ranch.

Today Temuco serves as the gateway to the major ski resort on the slopes of the Volcan Pucón and the resorts on Lago Villarica. It is an active regional service and market center, regional financial center as well as the administrative capital of the surrounding territories. Many people visiting the region make Temuco their headquarters, branching out to visit the lakes to the south, the Volcan Pucón and the Volcan Llaima, which last erupted in 2008. To the north is the rugged Park Nacional Conguillìo. Temuco is also still a major trade center for the Mapuche, and their arts and crafts are an important source of trade as part of the tourist market.

PUERTO MONTT: All cruise itineraries between Buenos Aires and Valparaiso stop in Puerto Montt. Be prepared for a full day of exploration, as this is the only opportunity you will have to visit the

Lake District. Puerto Montt is located at the southern edge of the Lake District, where the mainland curves east to where it meets the Andes and the fjord country begins. Puerto Montt marks land's end as far as road travel is concerned on the west coast of South America. Beyond this point the mountains meet the sea with sheer slopes and the deep-water fjords have drown all the remaining coastal lowlands. The city is located on Reloncavi Sound, which is a large bay extending inland from the Gulf of Ancud.

The city only dates to 1853, named for Presidente Manuel Montt. Like Valdivia and Temuco, Puerto Montt has a mixed population that reflects the strong influx of German and Slavic immigrants. Today it has a population of 218,000, making it the second major city of the Lake District after Temuco. It is well connected to Temuco and Santiago with a four-lane expressway. There is also rail service north to Santiago, but at present there is no passenger service south of Temuco.

From Puerto Montt it is possible to travel by secondary road, one that is rather rough, over mountainous terrain interspersed with ferryboat connections, south into the fjord country for just over 480 kilometers or 300 miles before crossing into Argentina where the road ultimately reaches Comodoro Rivadavia. But this is not considered to be a highway, but rather a rough track that is not lightly undertaken. Or once into Argentina, you can drive south on Route 40 and continue all the way through Patagonia to the southern border of Argentina. There are roads that extend back into Chile to Puerto Natales and Punta Arenas. There is another mountain pass route north of Puerto Montt that crosses into Argentina to the very popular resort city of San Carlos de Bariloche. This is less than a full day's drive.

Despite being at land's end, Puerto Montt is well connected by air to all major cities to the north, then by small planes to remote villages along the southern fjord coast. Because the fjord country is a tourist attraction for those who want to see spectacular country, journeys south for those who live in the major cities begin in Puerto Montt. There is even service connecting it with Bariloche and Buenos Aires, as many Argentine residents enjoy summer trips into southern Chile. For most people who come to Chile, the country pretty much ends at Puerto Montt, but there is still nearly 1,600 kilometers or 1,000 miles of rugged fjord, mountain and glacial landscape south to the southern tip of the Western Hemisphere, Cabo de Hornos, better known as Cape Horn, located on the island of Tierra del Fuego.

Puerto Montt is crowded with visitors during the summer months, both as a destination itself and as the starting point for more ambitious journeys farther south. Locally mined lapis lazuli is highly prized and can be seen in many jewelry stores in the city. This semi-precious gemstone is only mined in Chile and Afghanistan, sought out for its deep blue color. There is a moderate size shopping mall on the downtown waterfront, and many streets containing a wide variety of shops catering to locals and visitors alike. If you take a moment to look at the downtown architecture, you will immediately see the strong Germanic influences that are so pronounced in southern Chile.

Since your cruise itinerary will only give you one day in Puerto Montt, the big question is what to do. If you choose to remain in the city, something I would not recommend, there are few specific attractions worthy of your time. This is not to say that Puerto Montt is not a pleasant city because in fact it is. But you will sacrifice the glory of the southern lakes and volcanic peaks. Thus it is my recommendation that you either take an all day ship's tour or negotiate with a local taxi driver to take you around for an entire day. Arranging a car and driver/guide through the cruise line is of course the third, but more expensive alternative. What you want to see on a full day outside of Puerto Montt will not entail a great distance: The major regional sights are:

* Volcan Osorno - This majestic volcanic cone has only one rival in the world and that is Mt. Fuji in Japan. Osorno can be enjoyed from the towns along the western shore of Lago Llanquihue or by a drive to the base camp at the lower slope of the 2,500 meters or 8,200 foot cone. The mountain maintains a perfect conical shape and is snow covered year around. Photographs of Osorno can easily be passed off to those who do not know the difference as being Mt. Fuji in Japan. They are virtual twins.

* Lago de Llanquihue - The largest and most southerly of the glacial lakes. This lake is quite large, extending some 30 miles in length and over 24 kilometers or 15 miles in width. It is lined with small resort towns, fruit orchards and woodlands along its western shore. And the lake is backed by both Osorno and Calbuco Volcanoes, lending an aura of absolute magnificence to the scenery.

* Volcan Calbuco - The sister peak to Osorno and having erupted more often, its shape is not perfectly conical. Because of the severity of the 2015 eruptions, it is presently difficult to be able to drive to the base of the mountain, but there are so many vantage points from the lakeshore for viewing.

* Frutillar - This small resort city is only 20 minutes north of Puerto

Montt. It offers great lakeshore views, fine restaurants and a flavor that is a mix of Bavaria with Chile. Frutillar was settled primarily by immigrants from Germany, and it maintains a very strong Bavarian flavor.

* Puerto Varas - The major small city on the shores of Lago de Llanquihue, Puerto Varas has become the center of tourism with many fine, but small hotels and numerous excellent restaurants.

* Parque Nacional Alcerce Andino - This mountain park is beyond words with its temperate rainforests and rushing rivers, but it is mainly accessible via hiking trails and not an easy trip for most city dwellers.

* Parque Cultural Ayaltue - Located about half hour drive from Puerto Montt, here you have the advantage of hiking trails through beautiful woodlands and reconstructions of what life was like in the early pre colonial period.

If you choose to remain in the city, here are the major highlights that can be accessed quite easily:

* The Fish Market - Located along the pedestrian waterfront walk, you will see all of the many species caught in local waters.

* Catedral Puerto Montt - A beautiful and imposing main Catholic church for the city.

* Museo Historico de Puerto Montt Juan Pablo II - This is the local historical museum for the city and its surroundings, located along the waterfront on Diego Portales 997. It is open daily from 10 AM to 1 PM and then from 2:30 to 6 PM daily.

* Plaza de Armas - The main plaza in the center of the downtown, always lively with local residents.

DINING OUT IN PUERTO MONTT: Where you have lunch depends upon your activities. If you have a private car with a driver/guide, you will probably have lunch in Puerto Varas, which is the center of sightseeing for the region. If you remain in Puerto Montt, other than eating on board ship, there are several restaurants that serve traditional Chileno cuisine. My recommendations below first cover Puerto Montt and then Puerto Varas:

* ChocoLatte Cafe - Here is where you can get a quick cup of excellently prepared coffee or hot chocolate while walking around the city center. It is very popular with locals, and you may find that little English is spoken. It is located at Calle O'Higgins 167. They are open all day but do not post their hours on line.

* Chile Picante - This small restaurant in a semi residential neighborhood on the hillside above the downtown receives rave reviews for its authentic Chileno cuisine. It is open for lunch and offers fresh

seafood and many innovative dishes on a daily basis. You will need to take a taxi, however, it is not that far from the city center, located at Avenida Vicente Perez Rosales 567.They are open from Noon to 3 PM and from 7:30 to 10:30 PM daily.

*Pa Mar Adentro - A great seafood restaurant is what many visitors to Puerto Montt are looking for, and this is it. They have a wide selection of seafood dishes served with Chileno flair, some dishes coming with hot and spicy sauce, which is not that widely seen in Chile. It is located at Avenida Pacheco Altamirano 2525, along the shore but southwest of the city center. It is a bit of a walk, so I recommend a taxi. They are open daily from Noon to Midnight.

* Rincon de la Carne - Here you will find a meat lover's paradise for lunch. The cuts of meat are the finest and they are prepared with true Chileno flavors, served in a very comfortable atmosphere. Located at Pasaje Los Pinos 2001, you will definitely need to take a taxi because it is in the far northern suburbs of the city, but worth the effort to get there. Open daily from 1 to 3:30 PM and from 8 to 11:30 PM.

DINING OUT IN PUERTO VARAS: Here are a couple of excellent choices if you happen to be in Puerto Varas at lunchtime:

* Casa Valdes - For many this is highly favored because it offers a spectacular view out across the lake to both Osorno and Calbuco Volcanoes. And of course the cuisine is excellent. It is located at Santa Rosa 040, the main shoreline road north of the city center. And it specializes in fresh seafood prepared with a Chileno flair. They are open from 12:30 to 4 PM and 7 to 11 PM daily.

* Onces Bellavista - Located along the lakefront at Ruta 225 km 34.5, a bit hard at first to find. But it is superb. The food is traditional Chileno, their crema de chocolo is absolutely superb, as are their seafood dishes. And of course the view of Osorno and Calbuco are hard to beat. They are open daily from 4 to 8 PM.

SHOPPING: Apart from the normal souvenirs, the only serious shopping that you would find in Puerto Montt would be for fine leather goods just as is true in the major ports of Argentina. The major shopping mall in the city center, located at Illapei 10 on the waterfront is the Mall Paseo Costanera. The mall is open from 10 AM to 9 PM daily. Apart from the major named stores found in Santiago, it does have a local artisan corner where you can buy handcraft items such as woven wares.

* Angelmo - A strip of interesting shops and restaurants located along the shoreline between where cruise ships dock and the downtown.

FINAL WORDS: As previously noted, there is not much to do in Puerto Montt, thus you are really better off spending your last hour or so in town, but taking a tour into the lake country to at least see the landscape and the majesty of the two volcanic cones of Osorno and Calbuco. The scenery in the Lake District is especially beautiful and reminiscent of the American Pacific Northwest or Japan.

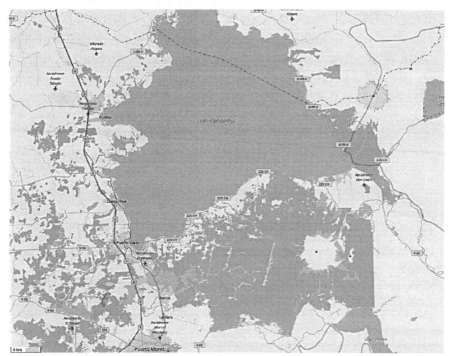

Lago de Llanquihue (© OpenStreetMap contributors

A map of Puerto Montt (© OpenStreetMap contributors)

A map of Puerto Varas (© OpenStreetMap contributors)

Calbuco and Osorno Volcanoes from just off shore of Puerto Montt

Overlooking the city center of Puerto Montt

The Germanic flavor of downtown Puerto Montt

The waterfront shopping mall in central Puerto Montt

The city center of Puerto Varas on Lago de Llanquihue

223

The main plaza in the heart of Puerto Varas

The Germanic architecture of Frutillar

The shoreline on Lago de Llanquihue at Frutillar

Osorno rising above the morning mist so like in Japan

The first minutes of the eruption of Calbuco Volcano April 30, 2015
(Compliments of a Chileno friend)

**Within half an hour the ash cloud is many kilometers high
(Compliments of a Chileno friend)**

VALPARAISO/VIÑA DEL MAR

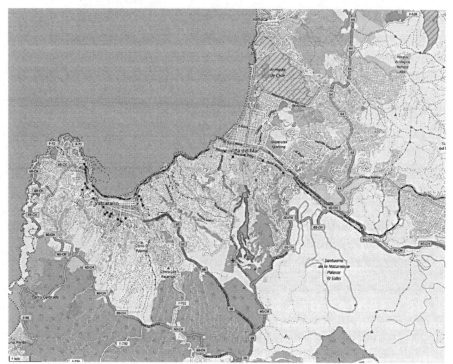

A map of the greater Valparaiso/Viña del Mar area (© OpenStreetMap contributors)

Cruises around the southern portion of South America either board in Valparaiso and end in Buenos Aires, or they travel westward from Buenos Aires to Valparaiso. Depending upon the cruise line, the cruise may be only one segment in a much longer cruise, the longest being a complete circumnavigation of South America beginning and ending in either Fort Lauderdale or Miami. Most often the major cruise lines will commit one ship to simply travel between Buenos Aires and Valparaiso for several segments during the period December to March, which is the Southern Hemisphere's summer.

If Valparaiso is your port of embarkation, you will have arrived in Chile by flying into Santiago. If Buenos Aires was your port of embarkation, you will depart from Santiago. In either case, spending several days in the Chilean capital is a must from my perspective. It is a dynamic city with a rich history, but a city that is on the cutting edge of modern outward growth. And its setting at the base of the Andes Mountains is quite spectacular. But the port of Valparaiso and its sister city of Viña del Mar should not be overlooked. I would recommend that if you are embarking in Valparaiso, arrange for a private car and driver/guide to pick you up at your hotel in Santiago and take you on a tour of Viña del Mar and Valparaiso en route to the ship. If you are not staying over in Santiago, and simply transferring from the airport to the ship after a long flight, you will miss seeing one of South America's great cities and one of its most interesting beach resorts and ports.

The cities of Valparaiso and Viña del Mar represent an important urban concentration. If one were to take the combined population of the two cities, they would represent a large overall concentration with a population of 930,220 people. Valparaiso is the most important seaport in Chile, and it is also a city with a rich history, but it did not begin to develop until 1791. The city grew in a rather haphazard manner, as its importance to the interior grew and there were more jobs in the shipping trade. As a result of its development, it is a city of unique character. Its houses are for the most part multi-story, of wood construction, brightly painted and they cling precariously to the steep hills that rise up from the amphitheater-like harbor. Some of the homes look like they are ready to tumble into the street below, presenting a look that appears to defy gravity. There are 15 funicular elevators that go from the lower streets, stopping en route to the upper edges of the city because many of the streets are literally too steep to walk. For the visitor, these funiculars provide awesome views of the city and the harbor. What makes this precariously built city even more amazing is the fact that it is located in a region that is so prone to serious earthquakes, yet it has survived for several centuries.

As a port city, Valparaiso is known for its many outdoor markets, similar in nature to those found in Italy. They are boisterous and colorful, selling everything from freshly caught seafood to locally grown produce. Although somewhat ramshackle in appearance, Valparaiso is a relatively safe city for visitors. Only the immediate port area gives the feeling of being a bit intimidating, and occasional pickpockets or camera thieves can be a bit of a problem if you are walking alone. For example, once when I was visiting the fish market alone to take photos a local police officer felt it his duty to stay with me and then walk me to my car because I was carrying an expensive camera. But this does show that local law enforcement takes particular care of foreign visitors.

The major role of Valparaiso is commerce. It serves as the primary seaport for the nation, especially for exporting of the agricultural produce that is so important in the central valley region. It is also the primary port for the importation of manufactured goods, heavy equipment and construction materials, vital to the ongoing success of the Chilean economy. Ships from all over the world can be found docked in Valparaiso's busy harbor. Cruise ships traveling the southern route through the Straits of Magellan all make regular port calls in Valparaiso. And most of the cruises around the southern tip of South America either originate or terminate here.

The city of Valparaiso merges on its northern edge with the fashionable resort city of Viña del Mar. This is a much newer city, founded in 1874 by wealthy residents from Santiago who wanted a seaside resort in which to cool off during the hot interior summers. This is a totally different city in its appearance than Valparaiso. It is a city of leafy gardens, manicured lawns, palatial homes and the beachfront is now lined with elegant high-rise condominiums and hotels. The actual city core is inland from the beach, adjacent to a richly planted park known as the Quaint Verger. This is the hub of the town's shopping and restaurants while the beach is more residential. Viña del Mar stands in total contrast to Valparaiso. All that separates them is a spur of hills that comes down to the shore, and once you round that hill the vista of a modern resort opens up. Because many service industry personnel work in Viña del Mar but live in Valparaiso, there has been a need for better transport between the two. This has been solved by a high-speed light rail link from central Valparaiso to central Viña del Mar, with a travel time of only 20 minutes.

If your cruise embarkation is in Valparaiso, no tours are offered unless your cruise line has a pre cruise hotel and tour package, but those generally are for Santiago rather than the port. If you are on a cruise terminating in Valparaiso, many cruise lines offer a tour of the port and beach areas while en route to the airport, but only for passengers having an afternoon or evening flight. And those cruise lines whose itineraries simply include a stop in Valparaiso and then continue onward will offer a variety of tours of the urban area, and possibly of the surrounding wine country. For those who plan to stay one night, I strongly recommend the hotels in Viña del Mar because they are superior to anything to be found in Valparaiso. If you are on your own and are planning to spend at least one night in Viña del Mar, here are the sights I would highly recommend you try and see by either arranging a car and driver/guide or negotiating with a local taxi:
* Cerro Concepcion - One of the best views of Valparaiso is from this high hill that can be reached by auto, but is more fun to visit on the

funicular and have your driver or taxi meet you at the top.

* Paseo Gervasoni - One of the most interesting streets to walk in Valparaiso because it is lined with unique and historic architecture.

* Valparaiso Historic Quarter - Around the main plaza in the heart of Valparaiso are the magnificent buildings from the days when this was the most important seaport in South America. It is worthy of at least an hour and is safe for walking.

* Plaza Sotomayor and Naval Headquarters - One of the dramatic architectural highlights of Valparaiso, located in the heart of the city.

* Catedral de Valparaiso - A magnificent and relatively large Catholic cathedral in very traditional architectural design, also in the city center. It is open to the public weekdays from 10 AM to 7 PM and 10 AM to 12:30 PM, but can be closed to the public during special events.

* Museo Maratimo Nacional - The very interesting Chileno naval museum where you learn about the role the navy played in the history of this long coastal nation. Open daily from 10 AM to 5:30 PM except Monday when the museum is closed.

* La Sebastiana - A rather strange and eclectic hilltop house that once was home to famous poet Pablo Neruda, considered a must when in Valparaiso because of its unusual architecture.

When in Viña del Mar, these are the attractions that I consider to be a must see:

* The Costanera - The magnificent eight miles stretch of yellow sandy beach that is the cornerstone of this resort city, today lined with high-rise buildings and presenting quite an impressive vista.

* Reñaca Beach - Just north of the city where the cliffs come close to the sea, this is a very popular beach backed up by great restaurants and shops.

* Avenida Peru - The grand boulevard that runs along the Costanera, a great place to walk and take in the sights.

* Floral Clock - A beautiful floral clock greets you as you come around the cliff from Valparaiso and into Viña del Mar.

* Quinta Vergara Museum - This onetime mansion is now the city's primary historical museum. There is also a local craft market here during summer. It is open from 9 AM to 6 PM daily, but closed Monday.

* Viña del Mar Casino - This is a must for those who want some nightlife and action, as there are few casinos to match in all of South America. The casino is always open.

Santiago has much more to offer for either a pre or post cruise visit, but please consider at least one day for Valparaiso and Viña del Mar, as it is well worth your time and money to visit these two cities.

DINING OUT: Viña del Mar being a resort city has a great variety of restaurants to suit every taste and budget. Once again I will only recommend the more up market restaurants that feature traditional Chileno recipes, as you should savor the local culture in a country where fine cuisine is so much a part of daily life. My restaurant recommendations are:

* Empanadas Mauricio - Nothing could be more Chileno than a good empanada, and a restaurant specializing in them is a perfect spot for lunch or dinner. In Trip Advisor, all of the reviews were in Spanish, and this tells you that the restaurant is clearly favored by locals. It is located at Calle Angramos in the northern district of Renaca, which means taking a taxi. But for a true taste of Chile, it is worthwhile. Open Monday thru Saturday 11 AM to 9 PM and Sunday 11 AM to 6 PM.

* Portofino - This popular restaurant located along the main road between Valparaiso and Viña del Mar is noted for its fresh seafood. However, on days when ships are in port, it often is crowded with bus tours. The Chilean sea bass, fish stew and conger eel are excellent. You also have a spectacular view over the cliffs at the pounding of the sea. Open Monday thru Friday 1 to 3 PM and 8 to 11 PM, Saturday 1 to 4 PM and 8 to 11 PM and Sunday 1 to 4 PM.

* Huacatay - Located just a few blocks south of the city center at Agua Santa 24, this restaurant is noted for traditional Andean cuisine from Peru and Chile. Their fresh fish and large lomo saltado sandwiches are exceptionally good. They are not open for lunch, so if you are staying over have your hotel check when they open for dinner, as many Chilean restaurants open late. Open aa:25 AM to 11:30 PM Monday thru Thursday, 11:15 AM to 2:30 AM Friday and 1 to 11:30 PM on weekends.

These are my only recommendations because the majority of the restaurants in Viña del Mar are Italian, French, Japanese or Continental European. This being an upmarket resort, locals and Argentinos who come are not looking for traditional Chileno cuisine.

PLACES TO SHOP: Viña del Mar has many fine gift boutiques and jewelry stores because it is a fashionable resort city. However, most of what you will see in the way of clothing for resort living is similar to what would be shown in North America or Europe. There are some shops selling traditional handcraft items along with the normal tourist souvenirs. Hand made jewelry in copper, wicker items, pottery and woven fabrics are among the items to be found.

Mall Marina Arauco with over 150 shops is the major shopping mall in Viña del Mar. The major department store is Ripley, also found in other major cities of Chile. The mall is open from 10:30 AM to 9 PM Monday thru Thursday, 10:30 AM to 9:30 PM Friday and Saturday and 11 AM to 9 PM on Sunday.

FINAL WORD: Please be sure to spend some of your time either before or after your cruise visiting Valparaiso and Viña del Mar. These are interesting cities and give you a totally different flavor of life in Chile than you see in the Lake District or in the fjord country. So many people who cruise simply either fly into their port of embarkation or fly home right after disembarking. And if you do that here in Chile, you will miss the real essence of the country along with also missing some incredible landscapes.

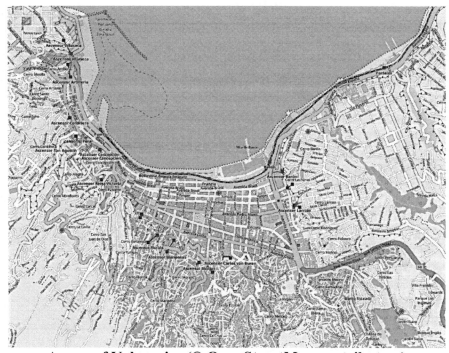

A map of Valparaiso (© OpenStreetMap contributors)

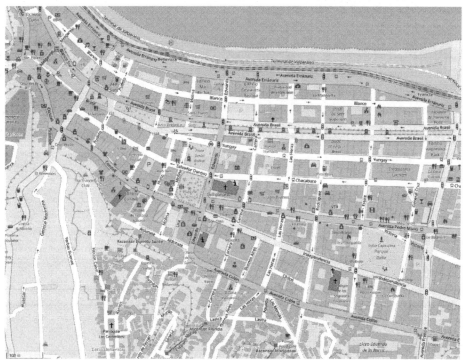

A street map of central Valparaiso (© OpenStreetMap contributors)

A street map of central Viña del Mar (© OpenStreetMap contributors)

Looking over Valparaiso from one of the funiculars

Valparaiso is a city of hills

Life is easy going in the Valparaiso hills

Chilean Naval Headquarters in Valparaiso

Old and new buildings merge in downtown Valparaiso

The colorful fish and produce market on the Valparaiso waterfront

There is so much animated street color in Valparaiso

Looking out over Viña del Mar

Weekend traffic in Viña del Mar along the beach

Viña del Mar is a city of fashionable high-rises

Viña del Mar's famous floral clock

The sandy beaches of Viña del Mar

SANTIAGO

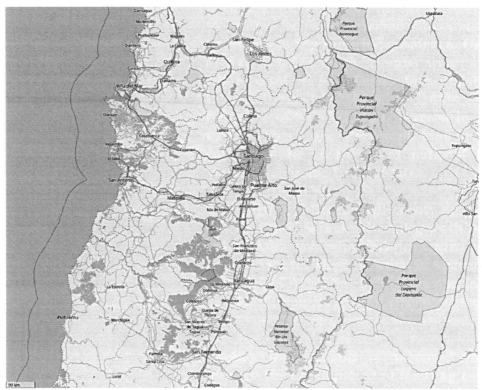

Greater Santiago (© OpenStreetMap contributors)

At either the start of your cruise or at its conclusion, you will be utilizing the international airport in Santiago for your overseas flight. Please accept my advice and spend at least two days in Santiago before going to Valparaiso to board your ship or after leaving the ship in Valparaiso, depending upon the direction of your cruise. Santiago is one of the great cities of South America. It is vibrant, exceptionally clean and blends Old World traditions with the 21st century, making it quite dynamic. Also its setting is very spectacular. There are several one-day trips that can be taken into the surrounding countryside that will be very memorable. I recommend a minimum of two days, but to fully appreciate Santiago, you should stay longer. The last time I was there (not my first visit), I stayed for nine days and still did not get to do everything I had planned. The flavor is totally unique and very different from that of Buenos Aires, so please consider it an integral part of your trip.

Santiago is the largest city in the nation and the national capital. Santiago is a modern city of 6,300,000 people, gently tucked into a valley between the coastal mountains and the high Andes. The site is spectacular without any question, as the Andes form a backdrop of peaks rising to the roof of the Americas. Aconcagua overlooks Santiago from the northeast, its peak rising to 6,960 meters or 22,834 feet, making it the highest mountain peak in the Western Hemisphere. Other adjacent peaks tower well into the 6,100 meter or 20,000 foot range, but hiding Aconcagua from view. This mountain wall is draped in snow year around, especially dramatic during the winter months. To the west, across the coastal hills is the important harbor of Valparaiso and the beautiful beaches of Viña del Mar, an hour's drive along the major motorway linking the coast to the capital. In the opposite direction, the ski slopes of Valle Nevado are only 40 miles outside of the city. Southwest of the city lies the Chilean wine-producing region, an extensive series of beautiful valleys in which some of the world's finest vineyards thrive.

The valley surrounding Santiago is blessed with a mild Mediterranean climate, one that supports scrub woodlands on the lower slopes and gallery forests along the many streams that descend from the high Andes on their way to the ocean. With very dry and mildly hot summers, the region browns up during summer and can be subjected to occasional brush fires, but during the winter months the land turns a verdant green. The many rivers provide ample irrigation water for agriculture, making this the most singly productive region in the country.

A BRIEF HISTORY: Santiago has an illustrious history, having been the first major colonial center founded in 1541 by Pedro de Valdivia. Although the indigenous Mapuche attempted to destroy the city, their repeated attacks only fostered greater Spanish resistance. The city was rebuilt and re fortified and ultimately became the heart of a vast ranching region filled with gracious haciendas. By the late 18th century, European architects began to beautify the city, expressing the wealth of the surrounding land. The Palacio de la Moneda, Chile's presidential palace, was built in neoclassical style, the largest such palatial building along the Andean front.

From early experiences with earthquakes, the Spanish learned how to build well with thick walls capable of withstanding all but the most catastrophic of tremors. The city has seen many strong earthquakes throughout its history, the latest one having occurred within less than a year of the writing of this text. Though none of the epicenters have ever been under the urban area, some have been close enough to cause major damage. All of Chile lives with the danger from earthquakes and volcanic eruptions. Today's modern high-rises in Santiago, and there are many, all are built with the latest earthquake resistant technology.

It was during the 18th and 19th centuries that Santiago saw the development of elegant parks and gardens, graceful bridges across the Rio Mapocho that flows through the urban area, the first railroad link to the coast and more public buildings to house museums, libraries and schools. As Santiago grew into the 20th century, it sprawled outward, and during the regime of Augosto Pinochet, encouragement of the private ownership of automobiles hastened the city's expansion. Today, Santiago suffers from both congested streets despite its expressways and it does have air pollution. Being located in a bowl surrounded by mountains, pollutants from automobile exhaust and factory emissions build up in winter when there is an inversion of warmer air above the colder air at the ground. If the condition sounds similar to Los Angeles, it should not be surprising. There are many visual parallels between the two cities both in terms of the physical environment and the urban growth. Both cities have attempted to combat the air pollution problem, but Santiago has not been as successful. The city does have an extensive Metro as well as commuter rail services, but the rise in automobile traffic continues with the economic prosperity of the country.

The city of Santiago essentially has a grid pattern with some streets that radiate outward from the city core. Today's Santiago has developed a north to south expressway, connecting to a westbound expressway that links the city to Valparaiso and continues east through the city center to the elegant suburb of Las Condes. On the outer edge of the city, a belt expressway encircles the bulk of the city proper. The city has placed several portions of the expressway system in the city center underground to minimize disruption of the surface configuration of streets. The central city lies to the south of the Rio Mapocho along whose banks there are numerous parks, museums and public facilities. Two primary hills rise up from within the city, Cerro San Cristóbal and Cerro Santa Lucia. San Cristóbal is over 823 meters or 2,700 feet high, rising up just north of the river, affording superb views of the downtown, the Andes and the entire urban region when the air pollution factor is minimal.

Santiago is undergoing a massive surge in high-rise development. For years the average height of downtown office blocks and apartments was under 20 stories. But with newer engineering techniques to resist the ravages of earthquakes, buildings now commonly rise to 30 and 40 stories, with the highest tower over 60 stories. East of the city center is Las Condes, the wealthiest suburban zone of the city. And Las Condes bears more of a resemblance to Vancouver or Toronto, Canada than it does any city in the United States. Fortunately the buildings are erected on larger plots of ground and are beautifully landscaped with gardens and trees. This is quite unlike the cheek by jowl high-rise construction seen in Buenos Aires or cities in Brazil. There is a more open and spacious feel to the new neighborhoods of Santiago. And the every present dominance of the high wall of the Andes to the east dwarfs the urban skyline, but adds great beauty.

The heart of every city in Latin America is generally a major plaza or great monument. In the case of Santiago, the heart of the city is Plaza de Armas, located just north of the Avenida Liberatador Bernardo O'Higgins, often referred to as the Alameda. The plaza is a meeting place for Santiago residents when they arrange to get together downtown. It is just south of the Casa de la Moneda, the elegant presidential palace, and office of the national president. Plaza de Armas celebrates the 1810 revolution against Spain. It is always thronged with people, and many of the shops around the plaza represent the very heart of the city's commercial district. There is a great degree of retail activity in central Santiago, as people still consider the downtown as the best location for shopping, dining and theater.

The many parks and squares in the central portion of Santiago reflect the strong European heritage of the city, the largest being Parque Forestal, which was designed by a French landscape architect. This is also the location for the elegant Museo de Bellas Artes, one of many European Neoclassical buildings that add an Old World touch to the city's central district. Across the Rio Mapocho, under Cerro San Cristobal is the Bellavista district. This is home to many of the cafes and fine restaurants as well as nightclubs, giving Santiago an after dark image that rivals that of Buenos Aires.

Much of residential Santiago reflects strong European influences as well as does the city center. Unlike México and many of the countries of Latin America, the residential neighborhoods (called barrios) are open, houses richly landscaped, but the majority are not walled in and totally hidden. However, many homeowners still have a small fence and gate in front of their homes for privacy. This holds true even in the middle and lower income barrios. The crime rate that is low compared to the other major cities of Latin America, and thus people of middle or upper income levels do not live in perpetual fear of being burglarized or kidnapped in their own homes.

Keep in mind that Santiago is not only the national capital and cultural and educational heart of the nation. This is a city that serves many roles; among them it is the transportation hub of the nation, the chief manufacturing center and also the country's prime financial center. Manufacturing districts are scattered, and the city is not generally thought of as being industrialized. On its eastern margins, Santiago has extended right into the lower foothills of the mountains, thus the only room for future growth is to the north, south and to a limited degree to the west.

The main highlights not to be missed while in Santiago include the following recommendations:
* Cerro San Cristóbol - The high mountain vista adjacent to downtown affords the best views of the city, but only visit if the air is clear. If there is heavy smog, your visit to the top of this mountain will be wasted. You can reach the summit by either car, taxi or the funicular.
* Plaza de Armas and the Metropolitan Cathedral - The true heart of Santiago steeped in history, as this is the core of the city in every way. The cathedral is quite grand, and the plaza is surrounded by numerous examples of 18th and 19th century colonial and neoclassical architecture. The cathedral is open to visitors during daytime hours.
* Casa de la Moneda - The presidential palace has a very sharp changing of the guard, but you must check with your hotel for the time of the ceremony. There is generally no admittance into the building, but it is still an important site to visit from the exterior. It was in this building that when revolutionaries stormed the interior, President Salvador Allende committed suicide, ushering in the Pinochet era.
* Parque Bicentenario - One of the most beautiful and tranquil parks in the city, located along the Mapocho River in the upscale barrio of Vitacura, offering great views of the city skyline.
* Parque Araucano - Located in the heart of Las Condes, surrounded by high-rise towers, this is a massive park filled with many outdoor activities. It is a great place for people watching, and it is adjacent to several major four and five-star hotels as well as the Araucano Shopping Mall. I enjoy sitting in the park on a summer evening and watching the color of the snow atop the Andes turn pink as the sunset develops. And yes it is safe to be in the park even as it turns dark.

* Parque Forestal - One of the largest parks with many hiking trails through beautifully wooded groves. This park is close to Barrio Lastarria, a district filled with cafes and pubs

* Metro de Santiago - Ride the metro if you have time, as many of the larger stations are artistically decorated and very beautiful. This is a popular means of travel and its lines cover the entire city. In the outer suburbs many lines operate above ground so it gives you a chance to see various parts of the city. But be aware of pickpockets, especially when the system is crowded.

* Providencia - A popular close in, yet upscale district that is filled with great shops, restaurants and night clubs. Providencia is quite lively at night.

* Mercado Central - One of the major public markets filled with colorful produce, meats, seafood and prepared dishes and people by the thousands, you get a great chance to appreciate the essence of food in the Chileno culture. The location is Ismael Valdes Vergara #900. The market is open Monday thru Thursday from 6 AM to 5 PM, Friday from 6 AM to 8 PM, Saturday from 6 AM to 6 PM and Sunday from 6 AM to 5 PM.

* Museo de la Memoria y Los Derechos Humanos - A museum that chronicles the brutal years under Presidente Pinochet, it is a must to truly understand the recent emergence of the country from that repressive era. It is located at Matucana 501. It is open from 10 AM to 6 PM Tuesday thru Sunday and closed on Monday.

* Museuo Chileno de Arte Precolombiano - Located near Plaza de Armas at Bandera 361, it has an excellent array of exhibits on the arts of the Pre Colombian cultures of the Andes. It is open Tuesday thru Sunday from 10 AM to 6 Pm and closed Monday.

* Museo Nacional de Historia Natural - A good museum to learn about the natural environments of Chile, a country where the physical landscape is so dramatic, and geologically still so very active. It is located in Parque Quinta Normal. It is open from 10 AM to 6 PM Tuesday thru Saturday and from 11 AM to 6 PM Sunday, and closed on Monday.

* Museo de Bellas Artes - A unique building with a massive glass canopy, and it has a good collection of Chileno art. It is located in Parque Forestal. It is open from 10 AM to 6:45 Pm Tuesday thru Sunday and closed Monday

* Grand Santiago Tower - Located at Vitacura 180, this tallest building in the city is not to be missed on a clear day. The observation deck on a clear day gives a 360 degree view of the city from a totally different perspective than Cerro San Cristobal. It is called Sky Costanera and is

on the 64th floor. The observation deck is open from 10 AM to 10 PM daily.

* Barrio Bellavista - A great neighborhood filled with restaurants and pubs and very lively, this is definitely an in place to visit.

* Estacion Central - One of the few grand old railway stations in South America, but this one functions. You might wish to take a ride on one of the local commuter trains to view parts of the city in passing, or take a day trip south into the wine country.

TRIPS CLOSE TO SANTIAGO: One incredible all day tour is to visit Portillo, one of Chile's major ski resorts perched high in the Andes adjacent to the border of Argentina. The drive on the Careterra Internacional is one you do not want to undertake on your own. This is the main highway between Santiago and Buenos Aires, but it only has one lane in each direction and once it begins to climb to the summit at around 14,000 feet, the highway snakes back and forth in dozens of sharp switchbacks that are not protected with guardrails. But professional drivers hired through your hotel are totally skilled at navigating this breath-defying highway. Even when you reach the summit, the mountains on either side are still rising 7,000 feet or more above you and have permanent snowfields or glaciers. A late morning snack of empanadas or a light lunch is possible during summer at the lodge in Portillo. Or you can return and detour slightly north to Termas Jahuel, a famous hot springs resort for a gourmet lunch amid vineyards and orchards.

Another mountain drive you can take is to Valle Nevado. This is a very popular ski resort perched high in the Andes above Santiago. Again you need a car and driver, as the road is exceptionally steep with many sharp curves. There are no guardrails and the drops often are thousands of feet. You want to be able to enjoy the scenery and not concentrate on the driving. This is an especially scenic trip and one you will find very memorable.

SOUTH OF SANTIAGO: Outside of the city, dozens of small towns serve as local service communities for the hundreds of farms and ranches that dot the landscape. The central valley region is actually a collection of individual valleys whose primary orientation is east to west, as major rivers and streams pour their snow melt to the South Pacific Ocean. In some cases, low hills separate the valleys, and in other instances one valley just seems to merge into the next. Thus the region is often referred to as the Central Valley of Chile, but it is not a distinctive single valley as is the Central Valley of California, although its agricultural role is very similar.

Throughout this region there is a mix of farms and large hacienda estates, as ranching was the older of the two activities to first lay claim to the central valleys. The smaller towns exhibit more of the traditional colonial Spanish architecture with a central plaza, church and government buildings. But even in these smaller communities, there is not much of the typical flat roofed, Spanish adobe type of construction that would be found in other old regions colonized by Spain.

The Rio Maipo is joined by the Rio Mapocho southwest of Santiago. It is here that the major wineries are located, set amid lush vineyards that are tucked into every fold of the surrounding hills. Although there are vineyards throughout the central valley region, this particular valley exhibits the greatest concentration of orchards and vineyards, making it Chile's equivalent to California's Napa Valley.

South of the Rio Maipo, the valley around the small city of Rancagua is another agricultural region rich in orchards and vineyards. This region is also known for its citrus orchards, as Chile produces quality oranges primarily for the European market. Farther south is the Valle Longitudinal, one of the few significant valleys that extend along a north to south axis, as a result of distinct topographic factors where the coastal mountains directly parallel the Andes. Yet these hills are continually cut by west flowing rivers making their way to the ocean. The towns of Talea and Chillán serve as additional agricultural centers, exhibiting a rich architectural flavor of the colonial era.

A trip south into the wine and fruit growing country is memorable. I say such a trip is an absolute must. Your hotel can arrange a private car and driver and make reservations for tours of several wineries with lunch at a noted bodega or restaurant in the region. This is one of the most relaxing and enjoyable ways to spend a day, seeing beautiful countryside, experiencing the importance of the vineyards and fruit orchards, passing through small agricultural communities and tasting great wines and food. This can be costly, usually around $300 for a full day car with driver plus lunch. If you team up with other guests and make arrangements to share the expense, it then is a bargain. But forgetting cost, it is a must do event while in Santiago.

HOTEL RECOMMENDATIONS: I always like to recommend the top hotels when staying in foreign countries. In these hotels you will find

English widely spoken and these hotels offer cars and drivers plus internal security. And they are located in the best neighborhoods. In Santiago, the hotels that I strongly recommend are:

* Mandarin Oriental Hotel Santiago - This is in my opinion the top hotel. It is located in Los Condes, and its round tower offers dramatic views in every direction. But I always insist on a high floor with a view facing east to the Andes Mountains. The hotel is absolutely superb, offering all the amenities you expect in a five-star property. Their dining room is outstanding. They have a beautiful outdoor garden and pool. And the level of service is impeccable. The hotel is located at Avenida Presidente Kennedy 4601. It is very close to great shopping, excellent restaurants and not far from the eastern end of the Red Line on the Metro.

* Ritz Carlton - Located in the heart of Providencia, this five-star hotel offers superb rooms, excellent dining and all the amenities of a great hotel. However, it is in a very crowded, yet upscale part of the city. The rooms are not able to offer great views because of surrounding buildings. But if view is not important, consider its great location close to the heart of the city, and in a neighborhood where there are so many restaurants and shops to be accessed on foot day or night. It is located at El Alcalde 15.

* Santiago Marriott - This modern high-rise tower is located in the heart of Las Condes, close to the Grand Hyatt. It is a typical Marriott property, borderline between four and five-star. It is less Chileno and more American in its ambiance, but does offer all the services that you would expect from a major Marriott Hotel. It is located at Avenida Presidente Kennedy 5741.

* Hotel Ismael - A smaller more boutique oriented hotel, located very close to the heart of the city at Ismael Valdes Veragas 312 close to Plaza Baquedando and the Red Line Metro. It offers excellent rooms, many with balconies and views of the Andes Mountains. It also provides outstanding breakfast. But being in the heart of the city, you will hear traffic noise, especially during the daytime.

DINING OUT: Unlike visiting a port of call while on the cruise, when you stay in Santiago you will be dining in your hotel or out for all of your meals. Santiago is a gastronomic paradise. Its restaurants are very international, but once again I am only recommending those that have a distinct Chileno flavor. After all you want to savor the tastes of a country that is known for great cuisine such as Chile. My favorites in Santiago include:

* Ana Maria - This unique restaurant requires a reservation, as you must be admitted after ringing their door bell, and you must be on the

list. The restaurant occupies an old, historic building just south of the city center on Avenida Club Hipico 476. The menu includes seafood, poultry and meat all prepared in traditional Chileno style. It also has a very loyal local following along with visitors like me. But it is quite pricey, and this again causes some to give it less than great reviews because they are expecting far too much. I guarantee great food, and that is what counts. The restaurant is open Monday thru Saturday from 12:30 to 4 PM and 7:30 to 11 PM, and on Sunday only from 12:30 to 4 PM for lunch. Reservations are a must.

* Laminga - Here is an excellent and well--established restaurant that offers a culinary tour of South America from its menu. The restaurant provides a true culinary experience, offering regional dishes from all of Chile and elsewhere in Andean South America. Seafood is a major specialty, but poultry and meat are also in abundance. The restaurant is in Barrio Bellavista at Avenida Constitucion 125. It is open Tuesday thru Friday from 1 PM to 1 AM and on Saturday from 1 PM to 2 AM and on Sunday from 1 to 6 PM. Reservations advised.

* Peumayén Ancestral Food - Located at Avenida Constitucion 136 in Barrio Bellavista, this is one of the five most highly rated restaurants in Santiago. It offers a wide assortment of dishes from all over Chile, and its bread selection is one of the favorites of its many loyal patrons. Hours are from 1 to 3 PM and 7 to 11 PM Tuesday thru Saturday and from 1 to 4 PM Sunday.

SHOPPING: There are so many places to shop in Santiago for just about every product imaginable. But for arts and crafts, there is only one place and it is the Centro Artisanal Pueblito Los Dominicos - This is the best place for a broad selection of Chileno arts and crafts. Located on Avenida Apoquindo #9085 and open daily from 10:30 AM to 7 PM/

As a major city, Santiago definitely offers plenty of shopping from large, fashionable malls to boutique shops. Like Buenos Aires, leather is a popular item for visitors, both in the area of accessories and clothing as well as fine quality locally made shoes. And when it comes to major brand name shopping, you will find all that you would at home, but possibly at lower prices. The major shopping venues include:

* Costanera Center - This is the largest shopping mall in Santiago, and its stores feature name brands you will recognize. It is located along Avenida Andres Bello at 2425, which is half way between the city center and Las Condes, along the Mapocho River. Frankly it is just a big shopping mall and nothing distinctive, but it does offer variety and quality. The center is open daily from 10 AM to 10 PM.

* Parque Arauco - In Los Condes on Avenida Presidente Kennedy between the Marriott Santiago and the Grand Hyatt, this large mall does cater to the more upmarket residential area it serves. It does offer variety, but it tends to be higher priced than Costanera Center. It is open daily from 10 AM to 9 PM.

* Patio Bellavista - On Avenida Constitucion between 30 and 70 in Providencia, but north of the Mapocho River, this is a well known place for shopping and dining both, with many local products available. It is open daily from 10 AM until 2 AM for shopping and dining both.

FINAL WORDS: Once again I ask that you allow yourself a few days in which to enjoy all that Santiago has to offer. Both Santiago and Buenos Aires are world class cities. The cruise between the two, actually between Valparaiso and Buenos Aires simply gives you a chance to savor two of the great cities of the continent. And they are very different from one another both with regard to natural setting, architecture and the way of life. If I had to choose between them, I would be hard pressed to make a decision, as each is unique and each is special in its own way.

The city of Santiago (© OpenStreetMap contributors)

The heart of Santiago (© OpenStreetMap contributors)

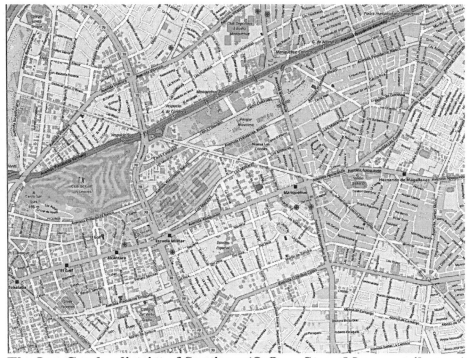

The Los Condes district of Santiago (© OpenStreetMap contributors)

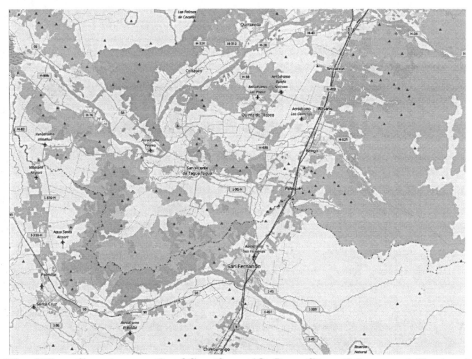

The Wine Country south of Santiago (© OpenStreetMap contributors)

Looking at central Santiago from Cerro San Cristobal

Looking at Plaza Baquedando from Cerro San Cristobal

Looking to the eastern suburbs from Cerro san Cristobal (Work of 3BRBS, CC BY SA 3.0, Wikimedia.org)

Avenida Bernardo O'Higgins in downtown Santiago

In the financial district of downtown Santiago

Casa la Moneda, the Presidential Palace

Plaza de Armas and the Metropolitan Cathedral of Santiago

Historic old Santiago south of Centro

Sunday morning in Providencia

A view of Las Condes and the Andes from the Grand Hyatt Hotel

View west down Avenida Presidente Kennedy in Las Condes

Sunset in Las Condes looking toward the Andes

High end residential apartments of Las Condes

High and los density living in the Santiago foothills

En route to Valle Nevada high in the Andes east of Santiago

Glacial Lago de Inca at Portillo in the high Andes

The ski resort of La Parva high above Santiago in the Andes

Valley Nevado is one of the major ski resorts above Santiago

The Colchaga Valley wine country south of Santiago

One of the many bodegas in the Colchaga Valley

The Colchaga Valley wine country south of Santiago

One of the many bodegas in Santa Cruz

FINAL WRAP

This text has given you a good opportunity to become acquainted with the ports of call and landscapes to be found on the popular cruise itinerary between Buenos Aires, Argentina and Valparaiso, Chile. The scenery is superb and the countries you will be visiting are progressive and in no way should they be confused with the many third world nations found in Latin America. Although Argentina, Uruguay and Chile have seen political turmoil in past decades, all three are thriving countries with healthy economies. These are essentially European nations with regard to their overall lifestyle and the percentage of people found in the middle and upper classes. Yes of course there is some poverty, but it is not all pervasive as it is in many of the third world countries of the region. And yes, economic problems have developed over the last few years with the world downturn in development. This has been most strongly felt in Argentina, but it has also impacted Uruguay and Chile.

It is nice to be able to travel in these southern countries without the worry about serious crime. And it is also comforting to know that food and water sanitation are highly regarded. Thus you do not need to worry about eating raw fruits and vegetables or utilizing tap water for washing and brushing your teeth. Most people do drink bottled water, as is true in North America, but primarily for the better taste and to avoid the chemicals used to purify domestic water supplies.

Once again, I highly stress the value of spending a few days in both Buenos Aires and Santiago at the start or conclusion of our cruise. These are two of the great cities of South America, and both have world-class character. I also strongly recommend that you take either private or group tours to visit some of the more scenic highlights, especially while in fjord country or the Chilean Lake District. After all when will you be coming this way again? For most people it is a once in a lifetime adventure. So enjoy!

ABOUT THE AUTHOR

Dr. Lew Deitch

I am Canadian and a semi-retired professor of geography with over 46 years of teaching experience. During my distinguished career, I directed the Honors Program at Northern Arizona University and developed many programs relating to the study of contemporary world affairs. I am an honors graduate of The University of California, Los Angeles, earned my Master of Arts at The University of Arizona and completed my doctorate in geography at The University of New England in Australia. I am a globetrotter, having visited 96 countries on all continents except Antarctica. My primary focus is upon human landscapes, especially such topics as local architecture, foods, clothing and folk music. I am also a student of world politics and conflict.

I enjoy being in front of an audience, and have spoken to thousands of people at civic and professional organizations. I have been lecturing on board ships for a major five star cruise line since 2008. I love to introduce people to exciting new places both by means of presenting vividly illustrated talks and through serving as a tour consultant for ports of call. I am also an avid writer, and for years I have written my own text books used in my university classes. Now I have turned my attention to writing travel companions, books that will introduce you to the country you are visiting, but not serving as a touring book like the major guides you find in all of the bookstores.

I also love languages, and my skills include a conversational knowledge of German, Russian and Spanish.

I am a Canadian/American and was raised in California. I lived in Canada and Australia. Arizona has been his permanent home since 1974. One exciting aspect of my life was the ten-year period during which I volunteered my time as an Arizona Highway Patrol reserve trooper, working out on the streets and highways and also developing new safety and enforcement programs for use statewide. I presently live just outside of Phoenix in the beautiful resort city of Scottsdale and still offer a few courses for the local community colleges when I am at home.

I would like to extend an invitation for you to join me on one of the Silversea cruise segments when I am on board presenting my destination talks. You would find it to be a wonderful experience, especially after having read my book on this area, or on the others I have written about.

FOR MORE INFORMATION REGARDING TRAVELING ON BOARD WHEN I AM THE SPEAKER, CONTACT, WESTSIDE INTERNATIONAL TRAVEL, THE TRAVEL AGENCY I USE FOR ALL MY TRAVELS AT:
www.westsideintltravel.com

TO CONTACT ME, PLEASE CHECK OUT MY WEB PAGE FOR MORE INFORMATION AT:
http://www.doctorlew.com

Made in the USA
Middletown, DE
13 May 2018